Suicide in Asia

T0083575

Hong Kong University Press thanks Xu Bing for writing the Press's name in his Square Word Calligraphy for the covers of its books. For further information, see p. iv.

Suicide in Asia
Causes and Prevention

Edited by Paul S.F. Yip

香港大學出版社
HONG KONG UNIVERSITY PRESS

Hong Kong University Press
14/F Hing Wai Centre
7 Tin Wan Praya Road
Aberdeen
Hong Kong

Hardback   ISBN 978-962-209-942-5
Paperback ISBN 978-962-209-943-2

Secure On-line Ordering
http://www.hkupress.org

British Library Cataloguing-in-Publication Data
A catalogue record for this book is available from the British Library.

Printed and bound by United League Graphic and Printing Co. Ltd., in Hong Kong, China

Hong Kong University Press is honoured that Xu Bing, whose art explores the
complex themes of language across cultures, has written the Press's name in his
Square Word Calligraphy. This signals our commitment to cross-cultural thinking
and the distinctive nature of our English-language books published in China.

"At first glance, Square Word Calligraphy appears to be nothing more unusual
than Chinese characters, but in fact it is a new way of rendering English words in
the format of a square so they resemble Chinese characters. Chinese viewers expect
to be able to read Square word Calligraphy but cannot. Western viewers, however
are surprised to find they can read it. Delight erupts when meaning is unexpectedly
revealed."

— Britta Erickson, *The Art of Xu Bing*

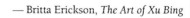

Contents

Preface

The idea for preparing this volume came after I attended the International Association for Suicide Prevention meeting in Stockholm in 2005. There I learned that over one million people commit suicide every year, and more than half of these occur in Asia (WHO 2003). However, very little reliable information is available for a good understanding of the multifaceted and complex issues involved in suicide prevention in Asia. Research on suicide in Asia is rare; it is undeveloped and under-funded. My guess is that 90% of worldwide suicide research resources are spent on 10% of the suicide population (mainly in the USA, Western Europe, Australia, and New Zealand). Over 60% of suicide deaths worldwide occurred in Asia.

In this volume, we make an effort to provide insights into an understanding of suicide, based on firsthand experience in our respective countries/regions. The book has covered the current suicide situation in eight societies in Asia. Each society has its own unique characteristics. Asia is a region under rapid transition; stress and depression have increased in the population, and both are closely linked to suicide. I frequently have been asked if the recent increase in suicide rates is related to the Asian financial crisis and unfavorable economic condition. Indeed, the economic environment can induce extra suicide risk, but an improved economy does not necessarily mean an automatic reduction in suicide rates, especially if the economic recovery benefits only a few as in Hong Kong, Japan, and South Korea. Although the stock indices have recovered significantly and have been at a historical high over the last three years in Hong Kong, Japan, Taiwan and South Korea, suicide rates still remain high in these places. An improvement in economic development certainly provides a more conducive environment for suicide prevention; however, it is neither a necessary nor a sufficient condition for the suicide rate to come down.

It is the collective wishes of all the contributors in this volume that through the publication of this book we will be able to have a better, evidence-based understanding of suicide in Asia and be able to establish effective suicide prevention strategies for the region. It is our humble and sincere desire that this book will encourage the respective governments in our region to make the examination of suicide a priority and eventually devise a national suicide prevention strategy.

On this occasion, I would like to thank the multidisciplinary team in the HKJC Centre for Suicide Research and Prevention at the University of Hong Kong. I am fortunate to work with a group of dedicated colleagues with a strong passion in carrying out evidence-based suicide prevention work in Hong Kong. I am grateful to the two anonymous reviewers of the draft manuscript who provided many stimulating and useful comments that have made the book more coherent. I thank Dennis Cheung of Hong Kong University Press for his advice and encouragement in the publishing process. I have also had the privilege to interact with many eminent suicide researchers around the world throughout the years whom I have learnt from. I also like to thank my family who patiently put up with the long hours that I spent in the office and away from home to engage in suicide research and prevention work.

The World Health Organization acknowledges that the principle of connectedness is important when designing suicide prevention programs. Restoring the connectedness between people and their community, workplaces, and families is not only the key to suicide prevention but should also be the guiding principle for stakeholders to work together especially in this region in which relationship is of great importance. I hope that our communities in this region can be reconnected to help those who are deprived and vulnerable. I am aware that not all suicides are preventable, but I strongly believe that we can make a difference.

Paul S.F. Yip
July 2008

Contributors

Anne Chao (Taiwan)

Dr. Chao is a Professor in Institute of Statistics, National Tsing Hua University, Taiwan. Her research interests include biological/ecological statistics and applications to health-related sciences. She holds a Taiwan National Chair in Statistics and is currently an Associate Editor for the journals: *Biometrics, Journal of Agricultural, Biological and Ecological Statistics* and *Australian and New Zealand Journal of Statistics*.

Audrey Chia (Singapore)

Dr. Chia, MBBS Hons (Sydney), FRANZCO, is a medical practitioner who is interested in studying suicide in Singapore, and has been assisting Boon-Hock Chia in his research in suicide research and prevention. She coauthored with B.H. Chia in some publications on suicide prevention research.

Boon Hock Chia (Singapore)

Dr. Chia is a psychiatrist based in Singapore. He graduated from the University of Hong Kong (1961), and did his postgraduate training at the Maudsley Institute of Mental Health, London (1965-7). Returning to Singapore, he worked briefly at the Woodbridge Mental Hospital before setting up his private practice. His interest in suicidology began in 1967, and in 1981, he gained his Doctorate in Medicine with his thesis "Suicide in Singapore". In the 1990s, he spent two years in Sydney working with Community Health Services. Dr Chia has penned three books on suicide: *Suicidal Behavior in Singapore*, *Too Young to Die*, and *Age of Despair*. Now semi-retired, he remains actively involved in suicide research, and spends his free time with his orchids, piano, golf and grandchildren.

C.K. Law (Hong Kong)

Dr. Law is a Postdoctoral Fellow of the HKJC Centre for Suicide Research and Prevention at the University of Hong Kong. He did his PhD on population studies in the University of Hong Kong. He is specializing in health economics and has received training from the World Health Organization (Geneva) on health promotion. He had also worked in the Hospital Authority of Hong Kong. He is conducting research studies on the socioeconomic cost of suicide, cost-benefit analysis and evaluation for suicide prevention strategies in Hong Kong.

David Lester (USA)

Dr. Lester is Professor of Psychology at the Richard Stockton College of New Jersey. Lester's scholarly research covers a broad range of issues in thanatology, resulting in the publication of 78 books and over 2,000 papers and reports, most of which focus on suicide.

P.C. Li (Taiwan)

Dr. Li is a Postdoctoral Fellow in National Tsing Hua University, Taiwan. His research interests are in the areas of public health, biostatistics and the use of capture-recapture experiment for improving surveillance and monitoring in public health areas.

K. Y. Liu (Hong Kong)

Dr. Liu is currently undertaking postdoctoral research in Columbia University on the social mechanisms of suicide. She had a bachelor degree from the University of Hong Kong and received her PhD in Sociology from the University of Oxford in 2007. She worked in the HKJC Centre for Suicide Research and Prevention at the University of Hong Kong and conducted research on suicidal behaviour among the general population in Hong Kong, deliberate self-harm patients presented to accident and emergency departments, and the epidemiology of suicide in Mainland China, Taiwan, and Hong Kong.

Manote Lotrakul (Thailand)

Dr. Lotrakul is an Associate Professor of psychiatry, department of psychiatry, Ramathibodi Hospital, Mahidol University, Bangkok. He obtained his medical degree from Chulalongkorn University and was trained in psychiatry at Somdet Chaopraya Institute of Psychiatry. He served as Editor-in-Chief of *Journal of the Psychiatric Association of Thailand* from 1996 through 2001. He currently serves as an executive committee of the Royal College of Psychiatrists of Thailand. His areas of clinical and research interests include mood disorders and suicide. He has various publications on these issues including the Royal College of Psychiatrists of Thailand's Clinical Practice Guidelines in suicide management and prevention.

B.C. Ben Park (South Korea)

Dr. Park is an Associate Professor in the Human Development and Family Studies program at Penn State DuBois. Dr. Park's scholarly effort focuses on suicide. In particular, his research on politically-motivated suicide has shed some light on the relationship between identity development and the logic in choosing such self-destructive behaviour.

Yoshitomo Takahashi (Japan)

Dr. Takahashi is a Professor of Division of Behavioral Sciences, National Defense Medical College Research Institute, Tokorozawa, Japan. He received his M.D. from Kanazawa University in 1979. He was given an opportunity by the Fulbright Commission to study suicide prevention under Professor Edwin Shneidman's guidance at University of California Los Angeles from 1987 to 1988. As a psychiatrist, he has conducted seminars on suicide prevention and published 20 books, about 300 journal articles and 120 book chapters on suicide prevention.

Lakshmi Vijayakumar (India)

Dr. Vijayakumar is the Head of the Department of Psychiatry, Voluntary Health Services, Adyar. She is also the founder of SNEHA, an NGO in Chennai for the prevention of suicide. She was Vice President of the International Association for Suicide Prevention (I.A.S.P.) for four years. She is a member of the WHO's International Network for Suicide Research and Prevention. She has various publications and is the editor of the book titled "Suicide Prevention - Meeting the challenge together" published by Orient Longman.

Paul S.F. Yip (Hong Kong)

Dr. Yip is the director of the HKJC Centre for Suicide Research and Prevention and a Professor of Social Work and Social Administration at the University of Hong Kong. He is a national representative of the Hong Kong SAR for the International Association of Suicide Prevention (IASP) and a fellow of the International Association of Suicide Research, a consultant for Beijing Suicide Prevention Service, a board member for Suicide Prevention Service (Hong Kong). His expertise is in population-health-related issues. His research interests include improving surveillance and monitoring of suicide statistics, adopting a public health approach to suicide prevention, understanding suicide differences between East and West and the effect of mass media reporting on suicide.

1

Introduction

Suicide has become a major public health issue throughout the world. Over a million people kill themselves every year, and more than half of these cases occur in Asia (WHO 2003). Suicide is especially a major concern in Asia due to its huge population and the relatively high suicide rate compared to that in Western countries. In response to the growing concern, the aim of this monograph is to provide an informative account of suicide in some Asian countries/societies to arouse more awareness of suicide in Asia so that more research and prevention efforts will be carried out.

Size and Magnitude of the Suicide Problem

Asia consists of more than half of the world's population and has considerable diversity in culture and socioeconomic development. The suicide rates are also very different: Japan and South Korea both have a high rate (about 25 per 100,000), Thailand has a relatively low rate (7 per 100,000), and Taiwan, China, Hong Kong, and Singapore are somewhere in between (15–18 per 100,000). However, it is the recent growth of suicide in these countries that is of particular concern. Suicide is the leading cause of death among young people (aged 15–24) in Hong Kong. South Korea and Japan. Taiwan have experienced nearly a threefold increase in suicide in the past decade. On the other hand, the suicide rate in Singapore has remained relatively steady. Thailand, a very religious country (Buddhism), used to have a low suicide rate (WHO 2003), but the rate has recently increased significantly. China and India are the two most populous countries in the world. It is estimated that about 250,000 and 100,000 people kill themselves every year in China and India, respectively. They have contributed to about 35% of total suicide deaths globally. Any suicide prevention effort in these countries would produce significant impact on the reduction of suicide numbers on a global scale. Also, 90% of these suicide deaths in Mainland China occur in rural regions (Yip and Liu, 2007). Similarly, rural regions in India have a much higher rate than urban regions.

Questions to be Answered

The suicide methods used in these eight countries/societies are very different too. Many questions need to be answered which are relevant to suicide prevention. For example, about 60% died from pesticide poisoning in China, so would restricting access to pesticides reduce the suicide rate? How does the rapid rate of urbanization in China relating to suicides? Perhaps because of the ubiquity of high-rise buildings in Singapore and Hong Kong, about 40%–70% of suicide deaths in these cities are from jumping from high places. Can we do anything about this to restrict the means by barring/fencing the high place? How can we curb the number of deaths from poisoning through charcoal burning in Hong Kong, which has been growing rampantly since 1998? Is the number of Internet suicides (people get to know each other via internet and plan to commit suicide together) in Japan getting out of control? How does the increase in suicide in Thailand relate to the spread of the AIDS virus? What happened to the suicide rate in Taiwan, which has increased by 300% since 1993? What are the roles of the economic and political environments towards suicide? Is there a different suicide pattern for different races in the city-state, Singapore? Are there any differences between the suicides in South Korea and Japan? What about hidden work-related suicides in Japan? Do religious beliefs protect people in Thailand against suicide? In response to all these questions, this monograph, which consists of contributions by leading researchers from various disciplines such as psychiatry, psychology, suicidology, statistics, social and public policy, public health, sociology, and social medicine, represents an attempt to share our experiences in their respective societies. It is hoped that insights into these problems based on first-hand experience can fill some of the gaps in knowledge about suicide research in this part of the world. The information would be useful in formulating effective suicide prevention strategies.

Organization of This Book

Here, we address the topic of suicide in various societies in Asia. We provide valuable updated epidemiological data about suicidal behavior in the East and compare it to data from the West. We, the chapter authors, use different

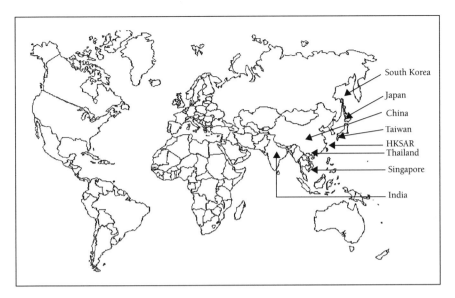

Figure 1   The locality of the right countries/societies in the book.

methodological approaches to the topic, based on our different professional backgrounds and academic disciplines, as well as on the different resources of information available. For each chapter, an overview of suicidality in the respective societies is given. A discussion of how the suicide behavior relates to social and cultural factors is explored, and some suicide prevention programs and/or efforts (if such exist) are reviewed. Eight countries/societies in this region are selected, which contain nearly 40% of the world's population. Each country/society is very different from the others in terms of its socioeconomic stages of development, religious beliefs, population size, gross national product (GNP), literacy rate, and suicide rate, etc., and so together they cover a diverse profile of Asia (Table 1). But they also provide a good representation of the countries/societies in this region.

The order of the chapters, which deal with different countries/societies, can be arranged alphabetically by country/society name. However, though this might be correct from a political perspective, the book as a whole would suffer from discontinuity as the chapters jumped from one society to another. Hence, we propose (as suggested by one of the reviewers), for the purpose of facilitating a meaningful understanding of the book, to arrange the chapter order in terms of the *geographical location* of the countries/societies, namely from north to south and from east to west within the Asian region (the order, therefore, is Japan, South Korea, Mainland China, Hong Kong, Taiwan, Thailand, Singapore, India). It is to be noted that some neighboring societies (which are geographically connected and culturally related in some way) are similar in terms of the suicidal behavior associated with social and cultural factors.

Table 1. A Socioeconomic Profile of the Eight Countries/Societies Chosen for the Monograph.

	China	Hong Kong	India	Japan	Singapore	South Korea	Taiwan	Thailand
Population	1,313,973,713 (July 2006 est.)	6,940,432 (July 2006 est.)	1,095,351,995 (July 2006 est.)	127,463,611 (July 2006 est.)	4,492,150 (July 2006 est.)	48,846,823 (July 2006 est.)	23,036,087	64,631,595
Population density (Pop per km²)	636	6,407	336	339	6,333	480	125	
Median age	total: 32.7 years male: 32.3 years female: 33.2 years	total: 40.7 years male: 40.4 years female: 40.9 years (2006 est.)	total: 24.9 years male: 24.9 years female: 24.9 years (2006 est.)	total: 42.9 years male: 41.1 years female: 44.7 years (2006 est.)	total: 37.3 years male: 36.9 years female: 37.6 years (2006 est.)	total: 35.2 years male: 34.2 years female: 36.3 years (2006 est.)	total: 34.6 years male: 34.1 years female: 35 years (2006 est.)	total: 31.9 years male: 31.1 years female: 32.8 years (2006 est.)
Population growth rate	0.59% (2006 est.)	0.59% (2006 est.)	1.38% (2006 est.)	0.02% (2006 est.)	1.42% (2006 est.)	0.42% (2006 est.)	0.61% (2006 est.)	0.68% (2006 est.)
Birth rate (births/1000 population)	13.25	7.29	22.01	9.37	9.34	10	12.56	13.87
Death rate (deaths/1000 population)	6.97	6.29	8.18	9.16	4.28	5.85	6.48	7.04
Marriage rate (per 1,000 population)	6.1 (2002)	6.0 (2004)	Not available	5.7 (2004)	6.4 (2004)	6.4 (2004)	5.8 (2004)	5.4 (2000)
Infant mortality rate(deaths/1000 live births)	total: 23.12 male: 20.6 female: 25.94	total: 2.95 male: 3.13 female: 2.75 (2006 est.)	total: 54.63 male: 55.18 female: 54.05 (2006 est.)	total: 3.24 male: 3.5 female: 2.97 (2006 est.)	total: 2.29 male: 2.5 female: 2.07 (2006 est.)	total: 6.29 male: 6.54 female: 5.75 (2006 est.)	total: 6.16 male: 6.97 female: 5.55 (2006 est.)	total: 19.49 male: 20.77 female: 18.15 (2006 est.)
Religion	Daoist (Taoist), Buddhist, Christian %–4%, Muslim 1%–2% ote: officially atheist (2002 est.)	eclectic mixture of local religions 90%, Christian 10%	Hindu 80.5%, Muslim 13.4%, Christian 2.3%, Sikh 1.9%, other 1.8%, unspecified 0.1% (2001 census)	observe both Shinto and Buddhist 84% other 16% (including Christian 0.7%)	Buddhist 42.5%, Muslim 14.9%, Taoist 8.5%, Hindu 4%, Catholic 4.8%, other Christian 9.8%, other 0.7%, none 14.8% (2000 census)	no affiliation 46%, Christian 26%, Buddhist 26%, Confucianist 1%, other 1%	mixture of Buddhist, Confucian, and Taoist 93%, Christian 4.5%, other 2.5%	Buddhist 94.6%, Muslim 4.6%, Christian 0.7%, other 0.1% (2000 census)
Unemployment rate	20% (2005 est.)	5.5% (2005 est.)	8.9% (2005 est.)	4.4% (2005 est.)	3.1% (2005 est.)	3.7% (2005 est.)	4.1% (2005 est.)	1.8% (2005 est.)

GDP per capital	$7,204 (2005 est.)	$37,400 (2006 est.)	$3,547 (2006 est.)	$32640 (2006 est.)	$28,368 (2006 est.)	$20,590 (2005 est.)	$27,500 (2005 est.)	$8,600 (2005 est.)
Total fertility rate (children born/woman)	1.73	0.95	2.73	1.4	1.06	1.27	1.57	1.64
Literacy (definition: age 15 and over can read and write/has attended school)	*total population:* 90.9% *male:* 95.1% *female:* 86.5% (2002)	*total population:* 93.5% *male:* 96.9% *female:* 89.6% (2002)	*total population:* 59.5% *male:* 70.2% *female:* 48.3% (2002)	*total population:* 99% *male:* 99% *female:* 99% (2003 est.)	*total population:* 92.5% *male:* 96.6% *female:* 88.6% (2002)	*total population:* 97.9% *male:* 99.2% *female:* 96.6% (2002)	*total population:* 96.1% *male:* NA% *female:* NA% (2003)	*total population:* 92.6% *male:* 94.9% *female:* 90.5% (2002)
Life expectancy	*total population:* 72.58 years *male:* 70.89 years *female:* 74.46 years (2006 est.)	*total population:* 81.59 years *male:* 78.9 years *female:* 84.5 years (2006 est.)	*total population:* 64.71 years *male:* 63.9 years *female:* 65.57 years (2006 est.)	*total population:* 81.25 years *male:* 77.96 years *female:* 84.7 years (2006 est.)	*total population:* 81.71 years *male:* 79.13 years *female:* 84.49 years (2006 est.)	*total population:* 77.04 years *male:* 73.61 years *female:* 80.75 years (2006 est.)	*total population:* 77.43 years *male:* 74.67 years *female:* 80.47 years (2006 est.)	*total population:* 72.25 years *male:* 69.95 years *female:* 74.68 years (2006 est.)
% HIV/AIDS	0.1% (2003)	0.1% (2003 est.)	0.9% (2001 est.)	less than 0.1% (2003 est.)	0.2% (2003 est.)	less than 0.1% (2003 est.)	NA	1.5% (2003 est.)
Medical health facility	Hospitals: 320,000 Doctor: 1.39 billion Physicians: 1,892,000 (1 per 687 persons)	Doctors: 1.52 (number per 1,000 people) Hospitals: 53 Physicians: 10,884 (1 per 625 persons)	Hospitals: 239 Physicians: 555,000 (1 per 1,853 persons)	Hospitals: 33 physicians 260,500 (1 per 489 persons); dentists 91,783 (1 per 1,388 persons); nurses 1,096,967 (1 per 116 persons)	Hospitals: 38 Physicians: 78,592 (1 per 606 persons)	Hospitals: 11 Physicians: 6,292 (1 per 670 persons)	Hospitals: 29 Physicians: 32,390 (1 per 697 persons)	Hospitals: 60 Physicians: 18,531 (1 per 3,395 persons)
Homicide rate/Crime rate (per year per 100,000)	9.23	0.63 (2005)	3.72 (1999)	0.50 (2000)	1.01 (1999)	2.18 (2004)	8.49 (2001)	8.47 (2000)
Leading causes death [suicide] ranking	5th	7th	Not available	10th	6th	4th	9th	Not available
HDI	0.768(2004)	0.927(2004)	0.611(2006)	0.949(2004)	0.916(2004)	0.912(2006)	0.910(2003)	0.784(2004)
Suicide rate (per 100,000) (2003)	18.8	18.6	10.5	27	9.5	24.0	14.1	6.8
Gini coefficient	0.44(2002)	0.525(2006)	0.325(2000)	0.379(2000)	0.481(2000)	0.358(2000)	0.326(2000)	0.511(2002)

Due to the sources of data and the professional background and interests of the chapter authors, the subjects dealt with in each chapter might differ, and sometimes this might be due to the unique profiles of suicide in different countries. Sometimes, only limited discussion on prevention in the eight societies is provided, which is due to early stages in its development. It is exactly the purpose of this monograph to highlight the issues in different countries/societies, hopefully stimulating the development of evidence-based suicide prevention strategies.

In the concluding chapter, a more detailed suicide prevention effort taken in Hong Kong is described for reference and reflections, and it is hoped that it can generate further discussion that will identify the culturally sensitive and best practice of suicide prevention for this region. We appreciate the sensitivity of the one-China policy. The term of societies, rather than country, is used to describe the suicide situations in the three societies, Taiwan, Hong Kong, and Mainland China. The concern of the suicide situations of the three societies is our ultimate concern.

We appreciate that there are a number of issues (including poverty, war, illiteracy, and natural disasters) that are going to be seen as higher priorities than suicide; however, as mental health has emerged as one of the main causes of death in the world, especially in regions of rapid transition, it is important to address this matter seriously, especially in those societies that have experienced a significant increase in the suicide rate in recent years. We make an impassioned plea for suicide prevention to be ranked as a major health priority in Asia.

Limitations

Only eight countries/societies are selected in the monograph from the 37 countries in the western Pacific region. Also, the problem of ascertaining suicide accurately in Asia provides an interesting contrast between those countries in which there is a coronial system of determining suicide, inherited from colonization and based on the British legal system (as in Hong Kong and Singapore), and those in which the suicide rate is estimated (e.g., China and India). If suicide prevention efforts are to be evaluated, then there has to be some way of ensuring that suicides are properly ascertained and monitored. However, to the best of the editor's knowledge, it is the best data that is available for the monograph's purpose. It is hoped that this monograph will provide the reader with a good understanding of the multifaceted and complex issues involved in suicide prevention in Asia.

2

Japan

Yoshitomo Takahashi

This chapter provides an epidemiological profile of suicide in Japan, which has one of the highest suicide rates in Asia. Suicide rates in Japan have increased significantly over the past decade, with a rate of 23.1 per 100,000 in 2003. Suicide rates have increased with age. The gender (male and female) ratio was about 2.6 to 1. Rural areas have a higher rate than that of urban areas. Depression is commonly found to be present among those who commit suicide and has been shown to be work related. Some implemented measures for suicide prevention are discussed.

Introduction

The average annual number of suicides for a ten-year-period between 1988 and 1997 was 22,410. However, the number became 32,863 in 1998, an increase of more than 10,000 in one year. Ever since then, the total number of suicides for each year has remained in the 30,000s. It even reached the record high of 34,427 in 2003. This means that about 90 people per day and about four people per hour end their life in Japan, (Figure 1). This situation should be considered as a grave crisis for mental health in Japan.

The degree of severity of the current situation of suicide incidents becomes more obvious when compared with traffic accident fatalities. People used to call this a "traffic war," and annual traffic fatalities reached 17,000 at their worst in the 1970s. However, as a result of long-term countermeasures, the annual traffic fatalities in 2003 decreased to 7,702. Although it may seem questionable to make a simple comparison between these two figures, since traffic fatalities only include people who die within 24 hours after the accident, the fact that the number of

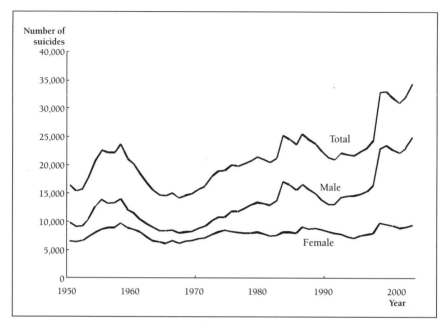

Figure 1   Annual number of suicide in Japan (NPA 2004).

suicide incidents is 4.5 times greater than the traffic fatalities in Japan remains striking.

The national statistics on suicide are made public, both by the National Policy Agency (NPA) and the Ministry of Health, Labor, and Welfare (MHLW). According to the Population Survey Report by the MHLW, the number of suicide incidents in 2003 was reported to be 32,082, which is approximately 2,000 fewer than the number announced by the NPA. The figure by the MHLW has been 1,000 to 2,000 fewer than the figure by the NPA every year. This might be due to the fact that a family doctor who knows well the deceased person and his/her family tends to avoid recording "suicide" as the clear cause of death on the death certificate.

Gender

In 2003, male suicide incidents were 24,963, and female suicide incidents were 9,464. The male-female ratio of accomplished suicides was 2.6 to 1. Although there are a few exceptions (e.g., Peoples' Republic China), completed suicide is more common among men worldwide.

There is no such great gender difference in the morbidity of mental disorders that are closely associated with suicide. Therefore, the question naturally arises of how this gender difference in suicide incidents can be explained. There are a few interpretations for this (Takahashi 1992).

(1) Females are biologically superior to males in their ability to control impulsiveness. Males tend to use more hostile, impulsive, and aggressive behavior in a problem-solving situation.

(2) In relation to (1), males tend to take more lethal measures when trying to commit suicide.

(3) Females have less resistance consulting with others when faced with problems and tend to take a candid attitude toward them.

Social expectations or norms, such as "Men should be strong," "Men should not show weakness to others," and "Men should not cry," are so strong that men cannot easily consult with others when they have a problem. It is obvious that men tend to bear problems by themselves. Biological and social factors, such as the ones described above, are thought to contribute to the outstanding gender difference in accomplished suicide incidents.

Age

Figure 2 shows the age distribution of suicide, in both males and females, in Japan. Elderly people have always been in the high-risk group. In 2003, 33.5% of suicide incidents occurred in the population of 60-year-olds and older. This phenomenon of the elderly population showing a higher suicide rate than the younger generation is not limited to Japan but is a general characteristic among developed countries.

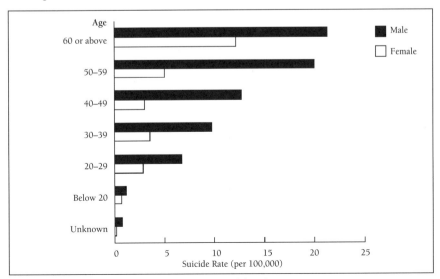

Figure 2   Age distribution of suicide in males and females.

In addition, 25% of people who committed suicide were in their 50s, and 15.7% were in their 40s. Thus, 40% of people committing suicide in Japan are in their most productive years. This also contrasts with the fact that suicide incidents among young people increased in the 1980s in many countries in Europe and the USA.

Meanwhile, the number of suicide deaths in their 30s was 4,603 in 2003, which was a 17% increase from the previous year. Although, people committing suicide in their 40s and 50s have constituted a noticeable trend since 1998, suicides among people in their 30s show an increase at this point and onwards.

Employee layoffs in the long-lasting economic recession mainly scarified people in the 40s and 50s. This tendency might impose a bigger burden to the younger generation in the work place.

Suicide Rates of Each Prefecture

The suicide rate of each prefecture is shown in Figure 3. Japan's suicide rate in 2003 was 27 per 100,000.

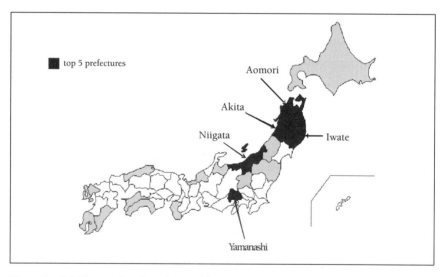

Figure 3   Suicide rate of each prefecture (above average rate).

Note: Prefectures with grey color show those with above average suicide rates and prefectures with dark color show those with the five highest suicide rates

Prefectures in the northernmost part of Honshu, such as Akita, Aomori, and Iwate, plus Niigata, have been showing a certain tendency toward a relatively high suicide rate. In these areas, this reality is contemplated, and people have begun to take proactive measures to prevent suicides in the community.

Prefectures that have a rapidly aging population also show high suicide rates. For instance, Akita Prefecture currently has a demographic composition similar to the one projected for Japan in 2020. On the other hand, statistics show urban areas as having a relatively low suicide rate; this is thought to be related to the fact that the younger population constitutes a greater portion in these areas.

In addition to the rapidly aging society, there is a report suggesting that prefectures with greater alcohol consumption and a higher rate of cerebrovascular disorders have a higher suicide rate. This suggestion is worth examining since both conditions are closely associated with depressive states (Conner et al. 2003). Furthermore, some have pointed out that the social climate where people have self-accusing tendencies when they are facing problems or where the majority of people think that life has become meaningless when they get too old to work is related to the higher suicide rate (Chiu et al. 2003; Takahashi et al. 1998).

Motives

According to the 2003 report of the NPA (2004) the most common motive for suicide was "health problem" (15,416), followed by "financial or personal matter" (8,897), "domestic trouble" (2,938), and "problem at the work place" (1,878). Among these, "financial or personal matter" has increased by 12% compared to the previous year, and the mass media have covered this sensationally as an outcome of the recession. Focusing on the generation and gender of the people who committed suicide because of "financial or personal matter," males in their 50s counted as the largest portion at 34%, followed by males in their 40s (20%). In terms of the detail of the motive, "debt" constituted a predominantly large portion at 56%, followed by "hardship of life" at 15%, and "business slump" at 12%. The number of people who committed suicide due to "financial or personal matter" was 1,703 in 1978, the first year the statistics for motives were taken, and this number has stayed between 1,000 and 3,000. The percentage of the total has been between 10% and 19%. However, numbers have continued to climb every year since it reached the 6,000s in 1998, and its percentage of the total hit the record high of 26% in the latest statistics.

It goes without saying that suicide is a complicated phenomenon, stemming from a variety of causes, and is impossible to explain with a single factor. It includes a process that can be called a preparatory state. Such a state is formed by the complex intertwining of various factors, such as stresses, mental disorders, a personality that tends to take in problems, family factors, etc. *In this situation,* suicide happens when triggered by some kind of an incident (a precipitating event). The precipitating event sometimes can appear to be just a minor event to an outsider.

In order to examine the cause or motive for the suicide, both the preparatory state and the precipitating event should be explored. It is possible that someone abruptly committed suicide by a trigger of an extremely grave event. However, in reality, the majority of suicides happen after a preparatory state has gradually been formed over a long period of time.

Since this data are collected by the police, who may not have enough training or knowledge in psychiatry and psychology, chances are high that only a rather superficial factor will be identified. It is also necessary to consider that the police make a point of picking out only one motive from various factors. For example, "health problem" is currently ranked the number one cause of suicide. Although this had been further categorized, in the statistics taken from 1999, into "suffering from illness" and "mental disorders including alcohol dependence," they have been lumped together as "health problem." This means that we do not know if someone was suffering from a physical disorder or a mental disorder.

Moreover, suicide due to a "financial or personal matter," even though attracting more attention since 1998, is undeniably a reason that more people have killed themselves in this long-term harsh economic recession. However, there is a possibility that the police who have been constantly surrounded by information about the unprecedented "great depression of Heisei," like any other citizens, were affected by the information when they had to categorize motives for suicide.

As mentioned above, categorizing each suicide case by a single motive can be a big problem. Therefore, it remains highly questionable to interpret motives for suicide based only on the statistics provided by the NPA.

International Comparison of Suicide Rate

Since it is not very realistic to include the statistics of all countries, only the figures of Europe, the USA, and Japan are shown in Figure 4 (WHO 2003). Although the year the statistics were taken of each country varied, all were taken around the year 2000 and should be relevant in examining the tendencies of recent years. The suicide figure of Japan was taken in 2003.

The reality is that countries with low rates of life expectancy have not paid enough attention to the issue of suicide because many people are dying of starvation or simple infectious diseases. Given this situation, countries that submit relatively accurate statistics to the World Health Organization (WHO) are limited to Europe and the USA.

Until the mid 1990s, the suicide rate in Japan remained around 18 per 100,000 people, which was a moderate figure compared to Western countries; it had been slightly higher than that of Germany and slightly lower than France's. However,

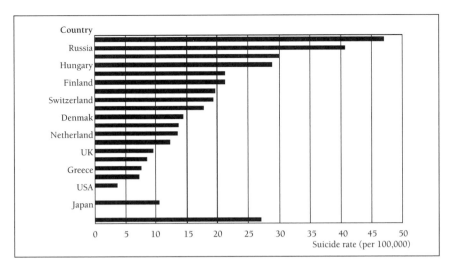

Figure 4   Suicide rates in Japan, Europe, and the USA.

Japan's suicide rate has recently increased and become about 27 in 2003. Although not only many Japanese but also non-Japanese believe that Japan has the highest suicide rate in the world, this is not true. There are countries with higher suicide rates than Japan. For instance, Lithuania and Russia have suicide rates of around 40 per 100,000 people.

As shown in Figure 4, the country with the highest suicide rate, Lithuania, is more than ten times higher than that of the lowest, Greece. What contributes to this difference? The close relation between mental disorders and suicide has been pointed out. However, even the most important morbidity of depression does not differ that much among countries.

There may be other explanations for such difference. First of all, according to the theory of Emile Durkheim (1951), an eminent sociologist in the nineteenth century, social ties could act as a preventive factor for suicide in countries where social ties still remain strong. Countries with high suicide rates also have the commonality that they have recently experienced dramatic social changes.

Furthermore, criteria used to judge suicide vary among countries. For example, in countries where social prejudice against suicide is strong, suicide without obvious evidence tends to be processed as a death with an unknown cause or an accidental death. Such a tendency has been recognized for some time.

In contrast, some countries, such as Hungary, have plenty of artistic works under the theme of suicide in its literature, theater, and music. People there take the common view that suicide is one means of problem solving that people can choose under certain circumstances. Within such a cultural sphere where people historically have accepted suicide, they have a lower tendency to hide it. Such a situation may be reflected as a relatively high suicide rate.

Implemented Measures for Suicide Prevention

As has been identified, the number of suicides increased rapidly by the end of the 1990s and remained in the 30,000s. In addition, it cannot be denied that a series of trials of suicide induced by overwork in the 1990s forced the government to take action and implement countermeasures for preventing suicides. There is a Japanese word "karo-jisatsu," which literally means suicide due to overwork. However, the so-called "Dentsu Karo-Jisatsu Trial" deserves special mention as the landmark case because it was the first overwork-related suicide trial for the Supreme Court in Japan (Takahashi 1998, 2003).

A 24-year-old man committed suicide in August 1991. His parents asked Dentsu, which is the leading public relations firm in Japan, for a full explanation on what actually happened before their son took his life. However, the firm did not comply with their request. The parents then filled a lawsuit against Dentsu, claiming that their son committed suicide due to prolonged work hours and psychological harassment.

As the link between long working hours and suicides had been recognized, the employer's obligation in providing a safe workplace was in question. The Supreme Court clearly stated that the employer assumes an obligation for creating a safe working environment that does not exhaust employees either physically or mentally. In addition, the Supreme Court pointed out that employers should take appropriate measures at the early stages if, unfortunately, an employee has developed such a disease.

In addition to this trial, the Kawasaki Steel Corporation Trial and the Otafuku Sauce Corporation Trial were also representative.

Responding to the results of such trials, MHLW took various countermeasures, such as a thorough implementation of appropriate working hours, revision of the criteria for certifying work-related compensation about mental disorders and suicide, and promotion of mental health in the workplace.

Figure 5 shows that the number of applications and certifications for work-related compensation for mental disorders and suicide eminently increased after the criteria for certifying worker's compensation relating to mental disorders and suicide were revised in 1999.

Moreover, research on the various preventive measures against suicides and the practical efforts to prevent suicides in the community, such as the council of advisers for preventive measures against suicides, began at the initiative of the MHLW.

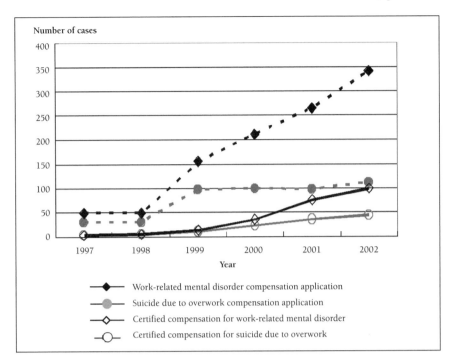

Number of cases

- ◆ Work-related mental disorder compensation application
- ● Suicide due to overwork compensation application
- ◇ Certified compensation for work-related mental disorder
- ○ Certified compensation for suicide due to overwork

Figure 5 Work-related accidents and compensations.

The author examined the expert witness reports in karo-jisatsu trials; 90% of the cases fell into the diagnosis of depression. It is especially applicable to males in their most productive years that they tend not to consult others when they are facing problems. In addition, they are afraid that it would become a negative factor for personnel evaluation if they admitted to having a mental problem in the midst of the recession.

Since knowledge about mental illnesses has not yet been disseminated enough, it is not unusual that someone who becomes aware of the problem ends up committing suicide before receiving appropriate care, especially among people in the prime of their life. There is a very striking linkage between depression and suicide. Once suffering from depression, one often experiences mood-related symptoms, such as depression and blaming oneself, and/or thought (volition) - related symptoms, including lower work efficiency, difficulty concentrating and making decisions. A variety of physical symptoms also appear, but very few people recognize any of these as symptoms of depression.

Depression could manifest itself in any sort of physical symptoms, including insomnia, lack of appetite, and weight loss. However, very few people seek psychiatric treatment from the start, partially because, in Japan, they do not want to admit that they have a mental disorder. The majority of people seek help from physicians who are not specialized in psychiatry; they begin by complaining of various physical symptoms. Miki (2002) reported which specialty of medical practitioners depressed patients consulted first. Two-thirds of depressed patients first seek help from physicians who specialize in internal medicine, while only 6% of such patients consult psychiatrists.

As a matter of course, the author is eager to recommend individuals with these physical symptoms having a physical check-up in order to rule out any physical problems. However, if someone experiences consistent physical ailments, despite the fact that repeated physical examinations have failed to find any medical conditions, they should consider seeking psychiatric help, looking at the possibility of having depression. Various effective treatments for depression are available today. Suffering from depression is not to be feared, but overlooking and leaving it untreated is the central problem.

Because a vast majority of depressed and suicidal people first seek help from non-psychiatrist physicians in Japan, the Japan Medical Association (JMA) edited and published "Suicide Prevention Manual for General Practitioner" in 2004 and distributed copies to all JMA members and medical school graduates (Japan Medical Association 2004). JMA also plans to hold workshops for general practitioners for diagnosing depression, treating depression, and preventing suicide.

As described before, many suicide incidents among trial cases of karo-jisatsu were caused by depression due to long working hours (WHO 2003). For information, the results of a recent survey by the WHO investigating 15,629 suicide cases are summarized in Figure 6.

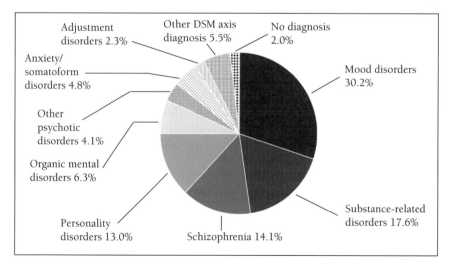

Figure 6   Suicide and mental disorders (all studies: 15,629 cases; 19,716 diagnoses; WHO 2003).

The survey shows that more than 90% of the people had been suffering from some forms of mental disorder before they ended their lives. Yet, only 10% to 20% of people received appropriate psychiatric treatment before their final acts. WHO emphasizes that suicides can be sufficiently prevented by diagnosing the underlying mental disorders at an early stage and introducing appropriate treatment, although it cannot assert that every suicide case can then be prevented.

Suicide Prevention in Japan

As indicated, the government of Japan has just begun to take a series of measures for suicide prevention after accepting the reality of the sudden increase of suicides beginning in the late 1990s. However, much criticism has come from the mass media, saying that not enough results have been produced. The author believes that a long-term commitment of at least a decade is necessary before seeing the effects of suicide prevention. It is premature to jump to the conclusion that these preventative measures are not effective after only a few years of trial. As mentioned earlier, the number of traffic fatalities, which had reached almost 17,000 in the worst year, has currently decreased to less than half. It took 30 some years to accomplish such a result. This is a valuable lesson. Even if one embraces the fatalistic attitude that says "it is impossible to prevent suicides," one should not reach such a conclusion before making enough effort.

It is essential to do the utmost to prevent suicides. However, it should also be pointed out that, in the era of more than 30,000 suicides per year, it is an equally important task to provide care to the survivors, people who were left behind with a psychological scar after a tragic suicide had happened.

3

South Korea

B. C. Ben Park and *David Lester*

South Korea's suicide rate has increased steadily in the past two decades, reaching 24.0 per 100,000 per year in 2003. It is one of the highest rates in Asia, and the pattern (by age and sex) is similar to that in Japan. This chapter examines the applicability of the theory of Durkheim, based on two dimensions (social integration and social regulation), for understanding suicide in South Korea. Implications for preventing suicide in Korea are discussed.

Introduction

One of the troubling issues in modern South Korea is the increasing suicide rate. The suicide rate in 1982 was 6.8 per100,000 people per year, but rose to 24.0 in 2003. Such an increase has been unprecedented in Korean history, and the trend seems to be continuing.[1] Over the past ten years, in particular, the rate has risen rather dramatically. The elderly are over-represented among those who engage in acts of suicide. For instance, in 2003, the suicide rate for people aged 60–74 was roughly 4.4 times higher than that of the 15–29 age group, and the suicide rate for people aged 75 and older was 10.6 times greater. It is important to ask why there has been such a sharp increase in the suicide rate in modern South Korean society.

---

1. The rate of 26.1 in 2005, for example, became available as we revised this chapter before printing.

Suicide is purely an individual decision and act for self-destruction. However, suicide is also profoundly affected by socio-historical trends. In this paper, we follow the tradition of Emile Durkheim (1951) in treating the suicide rate as a "social fact," as a product of aspects of social life that cannot be explained solely in terms of the biological or mental characteristics of the individual. Suicide must be seen in the context of trends and changes in the larger society. Although a range of explanations for the cause of suicide can be offered, the increasing suicide rate poses some important questions in the context of South Korean society, which has faced vast societal changes in recent years. Taking a Durkheimian perspective suggests that these changes are highly relevant for understanding the increased suicide rate in South Korean society.

Durkheim proposed that society is held together by a common morality. When a society changes rapidly, it is likely to experience a decline in this common morality. This weakened common morality creates a pathological social condition that weakens the bond between the individual and society. In this situation, called anomie by Durkheim, an old set of cultural values can become increasingly obsolete, while a new set of values has not yet been discerned and adopted by its members. Individuals can then become confused and cut adrift in their increasingly complex and specialized activities. Individuals who are confronted with anomie, according to Durkheim, may commit a wide range of destructive acts, including suicide.

In the modern world, there are strong indications that changing suicide rates are tied to the disruptions that societies undergo due to the forces of globalization and modernization. Studies in other countries have shown links between disruptions caused by social changes and an increased suicide rate. For example, Yip and Tan (1998) reported increased suicide rates during the period of 1984–94 in Hong Kong and Singapore, both of which are economically the most advanced in Southeast Asia. According to Yip and Tan, suicide rates among the elderly increased rather sharply, to about four to five times the average for the society in general. It appears that, as these societies became more deeply integrated into the global market system, the elderly became increasingly more alienated from the larger social, cultural, and economic structures, and so experienced greater anomie.

Clayer and Czechowicz (1991) reported that Aboriginal deaths by suicide in South Australia had risen from 10.1 to 105.3 per 100,000 for the period, 1981–88. Their study revealed that those Aboriginal people who "maintained traditional attitudes and way of life" (p. 684) were less likely to become suicidal (both fatally and nonfatally).

These studies indicate that disruptions in cultural traditions caused by major societal changes, such as globalization, are closely linked to high suicide rates.

Chandler et al. (2003), studying Native Americans, similarly suggested that people who fail to sustain self-continuity that connects their own past, present, and future are very much predisposed to an increased risk of suicide. More importantly, their study revealed that individual self-continuity is strongly associated with cultural continuity. Aboriginal communities who successfully preserve their heritage and culture, and who exercise some control over their future, have significantly lower youth suicide rates than those communities that fail to recover and maintain their own cultural heritage and the traditional governance of their institutions. Thus, people who are failing to sustain a workable sense of personal persistence in a transitional culture are at high risk of stress and psychopathology and have a greater likelihood of engaging in suicidal behavior.

Durkheim (1951) proposed a theory of suicide based on two dimensions: social integration and social regulation. Social integration is the extent to which the people in a society are bound together in social networks. High levels of social integration result in *altruistic* suicide, while low levels of social integration result in *egoistic* suicide. Social regulation is the extent to which the desires and behaviors of the members in a society are controlled by social values and norms. High levels of social regulation result in *fatalistic* suicide, while low levels of social regulation result in *anomic* suicide. Johnson (1965) argued that it was difficult empirically to distinguish between social integration and social regulation, and also that altruistic and fatalistic suicide are rare in modern societies. Therefore, Johnson simplified Durkheim's theory to the proposition that suicide is more common when social integration/regulation is low.

Lester and Yang (1998) operationalized social integration/regulation by using the marriage and birth rates of societies (marriages and births increase social integration/regulation) and divorce rates (divorces decrease social integration/ regulation). In regression analyses in 29 nations to predict suicide rates, they found that 22 of the regression coefficients for divorce rates as predictors of suicide rates were positive versus 7 negative; 9 of the regression coefficients for marriage rates were positive versus 20 negative; 12 of the regression coefficients for births rates were positive versus 17 negative. Thus, divorce and marriage rates were consistently associated with suicide rates in the manner predicted by Johnson.

In addition, studies have found that unemployment is associated with an increased risk of completed suicide (Park, Lee, and Kim 2003; Chuang and Huang 1996; Lester 1995; Lester 1994). Although the association between unemployment and suicidal behavior appears to be more reliable at the individual level, this association is statistically significant in some countries at the aggregate level (Lester and Yang 2003). For example, Park et al. (2003) found that unemployment rates were a significant predictor of suicide rates in South Korea for the period 1993–2000.

The South Korean Setting

South Korea can be characterized as a rapidly changing society. It has risen from one of the poorest countries in the world in the early 1960s (with its per capita gross national product [GNP] less than $100) to currently the world's 11th economic power. In the early years of this transformation, the effects of the changes on people's lives were limited by a reasonable level of cultural continuity. For example, even when people migrated *en masse* from rural to urban settings during the era of industrialization (from the late 1960s to the 1980s), they were still attached to traditional attitudes, such as the value of the extended family. This was evident in that people returned to their hometowns on special holidays to reconnect with their families and to reestablish traditional ties. The return-hometown activity still takes place today in South Korea but with significantly less intensity.

During the past decade, South Korean society has become deeply integrated into the globalized economic system. For example, in 1996, South Korea joined the Organization of Economic Cooperation and Development (OECD). As a result of this globalizing economic structure, South Korean society has experienced changes in many different areas, such as the social organization of work, new forms of business and trade, fashions, and global markets, with increasing accompanying social problems, such as increasing rates of crime, divorce, and unemployment, and lower birth rates. In particular, a major restructuring has occurred in the economy as a result of the financial crisis that brought the International Monetary Fund's intervention in the nation's economy in 1997. The increased number of contingent workers in corporate sectors has concerned people not only about the potential downward mobility for themselves but also about the effects on the welfare of their families. Today, families in South Korea are left with little public support to help them take care of their own members.

In addition, the rapid integration of South Korean society into the global economic structure has been accompanied by a shift in its cultural system, from traditional and collective moral values to Westernized, materialistic, and individualistic attitudes. Such a profound change in the nature of South Korean society affects some groups more than others. For instance, young people seem eager to break with the past and aspire to shape a future different from that which their parents and grandparents intended, while their elders seem to be passively disposed to the anomie resulting from the cultural discontinuities and contradictions. In fact, it is the youth who are proactively responding to the problems that their society faces, rebelling against the status quo and engaging in a new set of countercultural activities. Arguably, this youthful counterculture, which deviates from the traditional way of life, has become a binding force in providing meaning and a new identity for its members. Yet, for older adults, this emerging youth culture threatens the traditional, older values.

The present study is an attempt to explore the reasons why the suicide rate in South Korea has increased alarmingly, by examining the associations between the suicide rate and the birth, marriage, divorce, and unemployment rates. Gender and age differences were also examined as well as the methods for suicide.

Data and Method

Suicide, birth, divorce, marriage, and unemployment rates were obtained from the National Statistical Office of South Korea.[2] Data were made available for the period, 1983–2003. The suicide rates by gender for selective years (1983, 1988, 1993, 1998, 2003) are given in Figure 1. Suicide rates in South Korea increased over the period. In particular, this increase was most dramatic in the past decade — during the period of 1993–2003. The higher suicide rate is evident for both males and females, but the male suicide rate in South Korea has consistently remained substantially higher than that of females. The male-female ratio was about 2.2 in 2003. What happened in South Korean social structure during the period will be the primary focus of our discussion.

The data were analyzed using RATS (Regression Analysis of Time Series) (Doan 1990). The Cochrane-Orcutt method was used to correct for the serial autocorrelation in the data set.

---

2. The suicide data were compiled mainly on the basis of death certificates issued by medical institutions. The classificatory system, following the guidelines suggested by the World Health Organization, underwent two modifications in the past two decades (in 1993 and 2003), both of which involved more specification of the age group and the cause of death. These modifications, therefore, did not affect the way the suicide data were recorded.

It is possible that the data from the National Statistical Office (NSOSK) used in this study are under-estimates. The suicide rate calculated by the National Police Agency of South Korea (NPASK) is higher than that of the NSOSK. For example, suicide rate issued by NPASK was 27.4 per 100,000 for 2002, whereas the suicide rate issued by NSOSK was 19.1. The discrepancy between two government agencies may lie in the different methods of collecting the data. According to Lee Hong Shick, president of the Korea Association for Suicide Prevention, the NPASK report may be closer to the reality because, unlike the NSOSK data that rely solely on death certificates issued by physicians, the NPASK data are based on field investigations by the police that includes detailed accounts based on affidavits from family members, relatives, and friends, in addition to autopsy reports.

Given the cultural context in which self-destruction is generally perceived as a serious breach of Confucian teaching, and therefore becomes shameful to one's family, it is plausible to infer that some families use their social status to persuade physicians to record the death with a cause other than suicide.

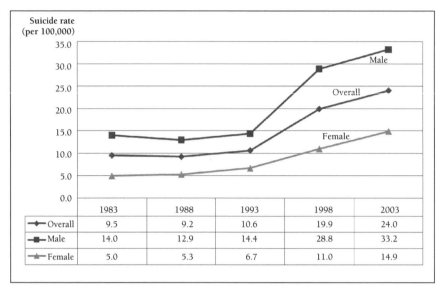

Figure 1   Suicide rates by gender.

Results

The Pearson correlations are shown in Table 1, and the results of the linear and corrected regressions in Table 2. For the simple correlations, it can be seen that a higher rate of births and marriages in a year was associated with a lower suicide rate (overall and for the male and female suicide rates separately), whereas a higher rate of divorces in a year was associated with a higher suicide rate. These associations are in line with predictions from Johnson's theory of suicide.

These results were generally supported by the regression analyses. In the simple linear (uncorrected) regression, divorce rates proved to be the strongest predictor of the suicide rate, while, in the corrected regressions, both divorce and marriage rates contributed significantly to the prediction of suicide rates. However, in the regression analyses, the sign for marriage rates was positive, opposite to that found for the simple correlations. Thus the role of marriage in predicting Korean suicide rates remains ambiguous.

Unemployment appears to be a significant factor only for the male suicide rate and not for the female rate. In addition to confirming the findings of the study by Park et al. (2003), which demonstrated the significant effect of unemployment rates on suicide in the South Korean social context, the present results document the greater impact of unemployment on male suicide rates than on female suicide rates. However, in the corrected regression analysis, the significance level for male suicide rates drops to $p = .06$ from $p < .05$. This may indicate that Park et al.'s study (2003) examining the period from 1993 to 2000

Table 1. Correlation Between Suicide Rates and
Measure of Social Integration/Regulation.

Correlations	Overall suicide	Male suicide	Female suicide
Birth rate	−0.84	−0.82	−0.86
Marriage rate	−0.85	−0.83	−0.85
Divorce rate	0.94	0.92	0.96
Unemployment	0.46	0.51	0.33

Table 2. Results of the Regression Analysis to Predict the Suicide Rate.

	Overall suicide	Male suicide	Female suicide
Regressions: simple			
Constant	−4.16	−4.00	−4.66
Birth rate	−0.17	−0.24	−0.06
Marriage rate	1.07	1.26	0.81
Divorce rate	5.30***	6.90**	3.82***
Unemployment rate	0.50	1.01*	0.01
R^2	0.90	0.89	0.93
Regression: Cochrane-Orcutt			
Constant	−14.97	−22.21	−6.92
Birth rate	−0.33	−0.45	−0.25
Marriage rate	2.14*	2.99*	1.29*
Divorce rate	7.54***	10.61***	4.37***
Unemployment rate	0.45	0.89#	−0.01
R^2	0.94	0.93	0.94

$p = 0.06$; * $p < .05$; ** $p < .01$; *** $p < .001$

reflected a period effect, during which the financial crisis in 1997 (that brought the International Monetary Fund's intervention) led South Korean society to experience unusually high unemployment rates for several years.

Age and Suicide Rates

Suicide rates by age for selective years (1983, 1988, 1993, 1998, and 2003) were available. As seen in Figure 2, as age increases, the suicide rates also increase. In particular, it is noteworthy that suicide rates among the older population have increased greatly since 1993. Similar to other Asian regions, such as Hong Kong, Taiwan, Singapore, and Beijing (Yip 1996; Yip and Tan 1998), the suicide rate among the elderly in South Korea was four or more times greater than the average. Also, the simple Pearson correlations between suicide rates and measures of social integration from ages 10–4 to 75–9 (not reported here) were consistent and

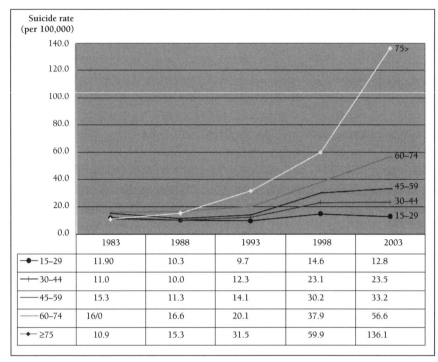

Figure 2   Suicide rates by age categories.

statistically significant only for those 30 years of age and older. The results suggest that older adults and elderly people in South Korea may be facing different social pressures and stressors than the younger generations.

Methods of Suicide

Data on methods of suicide for the period from 1993 to 2003 were available. As shown in Figure 3, the pattern of suicide methods over the past decade has not changed much. Poisoning by pesticides/chemical substances and suicide by hanging were two most widely and consistently employed methods of self-destruction over the ten-year period. These two methods accounted for 65.8% of the suicide in 1993, 74.7% in 1998, and 74.3% in 2003. The use of pesticides/chemicals, however, has increased from 32% in 1993 to 40.4% in 2003. The methods of jumping or lying in front of moving objects have also increased over the same period, while other means, such as drowning, crashing, and using fire, sharp objects, or firearms, have decreased. It is interesting to note that suicide by drugs or alcohol has decreased substantially. This drastic reduction could be due, in part, to the government regulation of sales of prescription drugs, such as non-opioid analgesics, antipyretics, sedative-hypnotics, and psychotropic drugs.

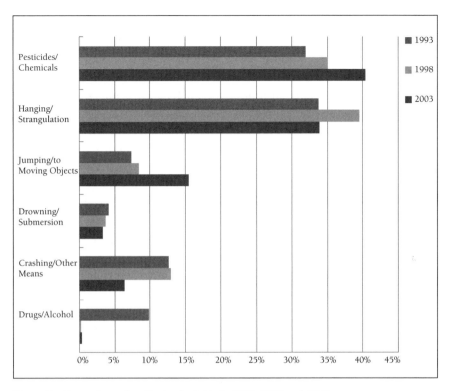

Figure 3 Proportions of methods of suicide in 1993, 1998 and 2003.

Discussion

The present analyses have indicated that some measures traditionally used to assess Durkheim's concepts of social integration/regulation are associated with the South Korean suicide rate in the manner predicted by Durkheim and Johnson. Divorce rates, as predicted, were the most significant predictor of suicide rates. Rates of suicide were also associated with the decreasing frequency of births, but less strongly. However, unlike findings in other studies, the inconsistent association between marriage and suicide rates may suggest unique cultural dynamics with regard to family relations in South Korea.[3]

---

3. A careful examination of family life as practiced in South Korea (and in other Asian countries) is needed. It has been observed that a large number of parents in South Korea have chosen to kill not only themselves but also their own children. A separate study would be required to deal with the complex cultural dynamics involving family integration/regulation. We hope to undertake such a study in the future.

The positive association between unemployment and suicide rates may indicate that working people's families are, in general, affected by economic stressors. The changing world of work, with the sharply increased number of "contingent workers" (rarely heard of before the 1997 financial crisis), seems to have affected males more profoundly than females. Understandably, the precariousness in the competitive job market may have created more stress on males who typically assume more responsibility than females for providing for their families. Employment for adult males in South Korean society has also provided an important source of social networking and personal identity. It is hypothesized, therefore, that with increased uncertainty about one's future (resulting from the globalized job market and the potential for downward mobility) an individual's sense of identity can be threatened, which makes it difficult to maintain meaningful, reciprocal, social relationships with others. Moreover, the lack of welfare programs designed to assist struggling individuals or families, thereby imposing a financial/emotional burden on other family members, might also intensify feelings of shame and guilt, which could potentially force the individual to consider suicide as an option for an escape.

Stronger associations were found for older adults and the elderly than for the youth, suggesting that the youth are relatively less affected by the societal changes in South Korean society. A similar pattern seems to be found in other Asian countries as well (Yip and Tan 1998). As described earlier, youth have "fresh contact" with history, and are more likely to be able to adapt to change than are the aged (Mannheim 1952). Older adults and elderly who try to hold on to traditional values may feel a deeper sense of anomie and social isolation. For those individuals, a common thread that connects their past, their present, and their future is not easily found. "Their own norms and values are no longer relevant," and they "are forced to respond to conditions that they have little or no ability to control" (Clayer and Czechowicz 1991, p. 685). As Chandler et al. argue (2003), people who lack self-preservation skills during times of change become more vulnerable to suicidal behavior. It is evident that, for many in the older generation in a changing South Korean society, a cultural shift results in a threat to and a disruption in their maintenance of self-preservation.

Nevertheless, it is important to note that, although anomie appears to be a principal social force alienating people from the larger society, for some people, particularly the elderly, suicide is sometimes chosen for altruistic reasons. The suicide notes that many elderly people leave behind indicate that the choice to end their own lives was to make a final contribution to their children. Their children are perhaps seen by their parents as struggling in the new realities of financial uncertainty, while still striving to fulfill cultural expectations of "filial duty" (the care of elderly parents). The burden of caring for aged parents typically falls on middle-aged children. It is plausible, therefore, to assume that the psychological and financial burden of fulfilling "filial duty" may be an additional cause of the sharp increase in suicide rates for older adults in South Korea. It is not uncommon in this cultural milieu to see elderly people voluntarily destroying themselves in an attempt to make a final sacrifice for their own struggling children.

The modern economic system in South Korea is not conducive to traditional family values, such as the veneration of the elderly. Increased competition and specialization demanded in the globalized market, combined with increased uncertainty about the future, has substantially undermined traditional South Korean family values. According to these values, the family is regarded as a social welfare and pension system for aged parents. South Korean families, in general, appear to have adapted to the changes that globalization has brought to them. Yet, in this transitional culture, some people apparently experience weakened ties to society and are unable to equip themselves with self-preservation skills.

Suicide Prevention

In an attempt to tackle the rising suicide rate in South Korea, the Korea Association for Suicide Prevention (KASP) was created in December 2003 by over 100 concerned citizens from all walks of life, and a national campaign was launched. The campaign aimed primarily to educate the public about the rising suicide rate and asked the media for help in reducing contagion effects by not making suicide cases the lead story, not repeating the story, especially for celebrity suicides, and indicating alternative ways of coping with unhappiness and stress, such as counseling, calling Life Line (a hotline), or seeking self-help groups. In addition, with the cooperation of other civic and religious organizations, KASP has organized the "Love Life" campaign to raise funds to establish preventive measures and sponsor various events, such as symposia and public discussions, on how to prevent suicide.

Since 2005, the South Korean government has acknowledged the issue as a social problem and has partnered with KASP in campaigning against suicide, offering educational workshops to mental health service practitioners and social workers about risk factors of suicide and intervention methods, providing on-line counseling to anyone who is in need, and monitoring the internet to identify web cites/ blogs that disseminate knowledge or harmful substances that can aid self-destructive behavior and promote Internet suicide pacts.

The challenge for suicide prevention efforts in South Korea includes many issues. Prevention measures have not been developed in the past. This lack of interest may have resulted from negative attitudes towards suicide and from the stigma associated with mental illness that is still widely prevalent in the South Korean culture. Many South Koreans do not consider seeking help from professional counselors as a way of resolving their problems. It is difficult to reach those who are in dire need unless they seek professional help. Because of the cultural belief that suicide is an individual problem, it is difficult to secure funds to expand programs to educate the public about seeking help for their mental health, as well as for training programs for other mental health service providers, physicians, etc. The current efforts should be regarded, therefore, as laying the base from which a more systematic and well-tested prevention strategy can be developed in the future.

The results of the present study suggest that the provision of support services for the elderly might be a useful tactic for reducing the suicide rate among the middle-aged and elderly population. It appears that the cultural tradition of filial obligation is not congruent with the increasingly competitive, specialized labor market of the modern era.

4

Mainland China

Ka Y. Liu and Paul S. F. Yip

Suicide is an important public health problem in China: it is the fifth leading cause of death, and over 30% of the world's suicide deaths take place in China. The substantial burden caused by suicide has not been well recognized. This chapter gives an epidemiological description of the suicide rates in China. There are many significant differences between suicide rates in China and the West, including a low gender ratio (male: female), a high rural suicide rate, and a high elderly suicide rate, especially among women. We discuss the roles of cultural and socioeconomic factors in explaining these unique features and their implications to suicide prevention in China.

Introduction

Suicide is a serious public health problem in mainland China. It is ranked among the ten leading causes of death, and it is the leading cause of death among women aged 20–9 (Phillips, Li, and Zhang 2002). Not only is China one of the countries with a relatively higher suicide rate, it also differs from other countries in terms of its unique suicide patterns (Phillips, Li, and Zhang 2002; Yip et al. 2005). In Western countries, there is a high male to female ratio of suicide, and suicide rates are generally higher in cities than in rural villages; however, the unique suicide pattern in China shows the exact opposite (Yip, Callanan, and Yuen 2000). Also, in some Western countries, such as Canada, the USA, Australia, and the UK, suicide rates in elderly males are two to three times the average suicide rate (WHO 2003). In China, the discrepancy between the average and elderly suicide rates are even more evident and the elderly female suicide rate is high (Yip et al.

2005). Not only is the epidemiological profile of suicide in China very different from their Western counterparts, they are also quite different from neighboring Asian countries. This chapter reports the epidemiological profile of suicide in China based on detailed mortality statistics provided by the Ministry of Health of China as well as data from Shanghai. We examine suicide rates based on age, gender, urbanity, and marital status and compare the results with findings from the West to highlight the similarities and differences between China and other countries.

Data and Methods

Suicide Data in Mainland China

Mortality statistics in China were very limited before the 1970s: all statistics concerning age or causes of death were unreported (Banister and Preston 1981). Since the 1970s, the Chinese government has realized the importance of statistics in informing national policies and improved the reporting systems. Currently there are two sources of information for causes of death and mortality statistics; one is the Ministry of Health (MOH) of China's Injury and Death Surveillance System; the other is the National Disease Surveillance Points (DSP) system. Both two systems rely on mortality statistics of sample areas and use the International Classification of Diseases, Ninth Revision (ICD-9) for cause of death classification.

These two monitoring systems each have their strengths. The DSP system is more representative than the MOH system because the MOH sample locations are mostly found in more developed areas like the coastal regions. On the other hand, the MOH has a larger sample size than the DSP. The former includes 10% of the population (approximately 100 million people), whereas the latter includes 1% of the population (approximately ten million people). Although the two systems have their own weaknesses, they both provide similar estimates concerning the mortality in China and can generally reflect the death rate, cause of deaths, and mortality trends in China. Estimates of suicide rate in 1990 based on the MOH and DSH system are similar: the estimate based on the MOH data was 18.8 per 100,000, and the estimate based on the DSP was 18.6 per 100,000. It suggests the mortality statistics based on these two systems are largely comparable.

This chapter primarily used the data provided by the MOH system, examining the trends of national, regional, gender- and age-specific suicide rates, and male to female ratios of suicide in China for the period 1990 to 2001. This MOH system collects data from 33 cities (urban regions) and 85 rural regions. The cities were categorized into large, medium, and small. A large city is one that has a population size of one million and above. There are 13 such cities in the MOH system (e.g., Beijing, Shanghai, Guangzhou, Cheng Du and Xian). A medium to small city is one with a population size of below one million and there are 19 such cities (e.g., Su Zhou, San Ming, Zi Gong, and Gwei Lin). Rural regions are divided into three types according to the social economic status of the area: Class 1 is an area that is relatively wealthy (e.g., Zu Zhou and Jie Jiang); Class 2 is an area that is considered sufficient (e.g., Hu Nan and Xi Cuan); and Class 3 is an area that is considered underprivileged (e.g., Gwei Zhou, Gan Su, and An Hui).

The data that the MOH collects are mainly derived from the death registration cards that medical professionals fill out when a death is reported. The death registration cards contain basic information about the deceased and the cause of death. There are a number of cards that are filled out by non-medical professionals; but the number of death registration cards filled out by non-medical professionals has been declining in recent years. On receiving the death registration card, family members of the deceased bring the card to the National Guard District Office to report the death and cancel the deceased's registration in the respective district. The death registration cards are then collected by the regional Health and Immunization Department officers from the National Guard District Offices at the beginning of every month. The officers then record and code each death according to the ICD-9 and produce the monthly mortality statistics. If the cause of death is questionable, and if the death registration card does not fulfill certain requirements, the Health and Immunization officers will conduct house visits for further investigation. At the end of each year, the annual mortality statistics will be compiled, with breakdowns in age, gender, district, and cause of death. Annual mortality rates are calculated based on the mid-year population size of each district.

There are two potential sources of underreporting of suicides in the official mortality statistics: unreported deaths and suicides that have been misclassified as death by other causes. Various adjustments have been made to the MOH and DSP systems' statistics to estimate the suicide rate in China. For instance, the Global Burden of Disease (GBD) study made two adjustments to the DSP system's mortality statistics and yielded an estimate of 340,000 suicides, or 30.3 per 100,000, in 1990 (Murray and Lopez 1996). The first adjustment concerned unreported death, the second potentially misclassified suicides, such as "unknown cause of death" and "other violent deaths." Phillips et al. (1999), however, argue that the GBD study overestimated the suicide rate in China. They argue that the GBD's adjustment concerning the potentially misclassified suicides did not represent the actual situation in China. The GBD study's estimate was 24.5 per 100,000 after adjusting only for unreported deaths, which was around 3% of all deaths. Phillips and colleagues used DSP data between 1990 and 1994 and estimated the suicide rate in China was 28.7 per 100,000 for that period (Phillips, Liu, and Zhang 1999).

The current study employs data kindly made available by the MOH for research purposes only. To avoid underrepresentation from only using the MOH system, some of the detailed suicide data were made available from Shanghai to examine the marital status and the method of suicide in China.

Results

Comparison of Suicide Rates in China and Other Countries

The GBD study estimated the average suicide rate in other countries and areas in the world to be around 10.7 per 100,000. Hence, it suggests that the suicide rate in China should be at least twice as high as suicide rates in other countries and areas in the world. Table 1 lists the suicide rates of 14 countries and areas in the world, which are spread across North America, Europe, Australia, and Asia. Compared with these 14, China has a relatively high rural suicide rate, which is not only higher than Western countries, but also higher than its Asian counterparts, such as Singapore and Japan. However, it should be noted that the suicide rate in the urban areas is lower than in other city states, such as Singapore and Hong Kong.

Table 1. Suicide Rates per 100,000 in Fourteen Countries and Societies.

Countries/areas	Year	Overall	Male	Female	Gender ratio
USA	2001	10.7	17.6	4.1	4.3
Canada	2001	11.9	18.7	5.2	3.6
England	2001	6.9	10.8	3.1	3.5
Ireland	2003	10.3	16.9	3.7	4.6
Greece	2003	3.4	5.6	1.2	4.7
Finland	2003	20.6	31.9	9.8	3.3
Italy	2002	7.1	11.4	3.1	3.7
Germany	2003	13.1	19.6	6.8	2.9
Australia	2001	12.7	20.1	5.3	3.8
New Zealand	2000	11.9	19.8	4.2	4.7
Japan	2002	23.8	35.2	12.8	2.8
Singapore	2002	9.5	11.4	7.6	1.5
Hong Kong	2002	15.3	20.7	10.2	2.0
Taiwan	2002	12.7	13.7	8.8	1.9

The data from the MOH system also arrived at the same conclusion. The death statistics provided to the WHO China was derived from the MOH system. Out of the 39 countries in the world that provided data to the WHO, China ranked second highest in suicide rates for the age group 15–25, and ranked third for the age group 65–74.

Trends in Suicide Rates

Although there was disagreement on the absolute values of suicide rates in China, the trend, for certain, is of particular importance in analyzing suicides in China (Yip et al. 2005). Figure 1 gives the *crude* suicide rates by gender and by urban and rural regions from 1991 to 2001, based on the MOH data. The unadjusted suicide rates for both males and females showed downward trends. Urban male suicide rates decreased by 27% from 8.3 to 5.8 per 100,000 between 1991 and 2001. Compared with the male suicide rates, the urban female suicide rates declined more substantially, from 9.9 to 5.3 per 100,000 between 1991 and 2001, a drop of 46%. In the rural regions, male suicide rates decreased by 23%, from 25.3 to 19.6 per 100,000 during the same period. Rural female suicide rates deceased by 33%, from 33 per 100,000 in 1991 to 22.0 per 100,000 in 2001.

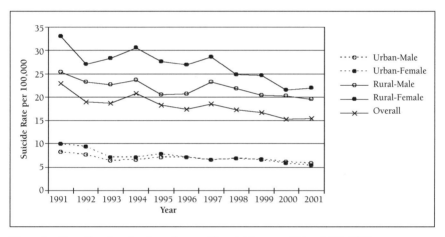

Figure 1   Overall and regional gender-specific suicide rates, China, 1991–2001.

Note: An update to year 2001 of the figures reported in Yip et al. (2005). Suicide rates in China during a decade of rapid social changes. *Social Psychiatry and Psychiatric Epidemiology*, 40, 792–8.

It should be noted that a country's suicide rates are affected by the age structure of the population. As those 65 years and older have a significantly higher suicide rate than any other age group, the aging population may cause the crude suicide rate to increase. In the 1990s, China's population experienced rapid aging: the percentage of people 65 years and above increased from 5.6% in 1990 to 7.0% in 2001. Therefore, greater decreases should be found in the suicide rates standardized to the population age structure in 1991.

As noted by Yip et al. (2005), there are substantial differences in the age groups that showed the largest decreases in suicide rates in the rural and urban areas. In the urban areas, the two older age groups (60–9 and 70+) showed the largest significant decrease in suicide rates. In the rural areas, the suicide rates of the older age groups fluctuated but remained at high levels for the period. The groups that showed the largest decrease in suicide rates were the younger groups (10–9 and 20–9) in rural areas, particularly among rural women aged 20–9 (Figure 2).

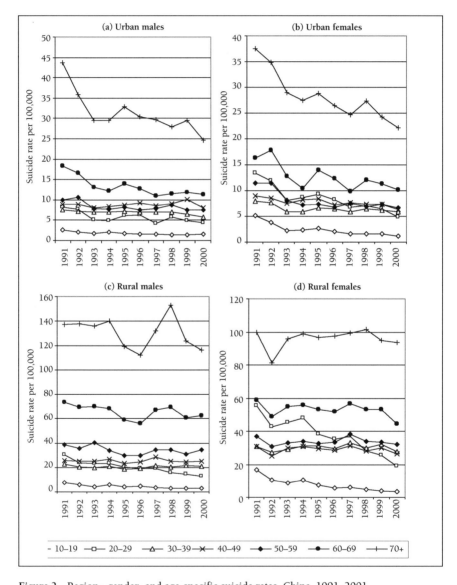

Figure 2   Region-, gender- and age-specific suicide rates, China, 1991–2001.

Note: Adapted from Yip P. S. F., K.Y. Liu, J. Hu, and X. M. Song . (2005). Suicide rates in China during a decade of rapid social changes. *Social Psychiatry and Psychiatric Epidemiology.* 40:792–8.

Further Breakdown of Suicide Rates by Urbanity

Figures 3, 4, and Table 2 show age- and gender-specific suicide rates in large urban areas, middle/small urban areas, Class 1 rural areas (i.e., wealthier areas), Class 2 rural areas (i.e., sufficient areas), and Class 3 rural areas (i.e., underprivileged areas) in 2001. Across all regions, suicide rates tend to increase with age, and suicide rates among the elderly are significantly higher than their younger counterparts.

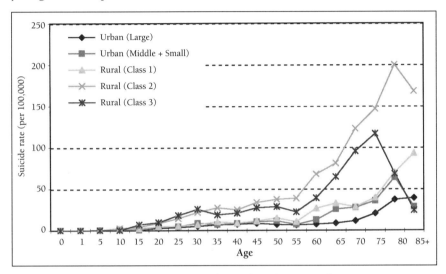

Figure 3   Age-specific male suicide rates, urban and rural regions, China, 2001.

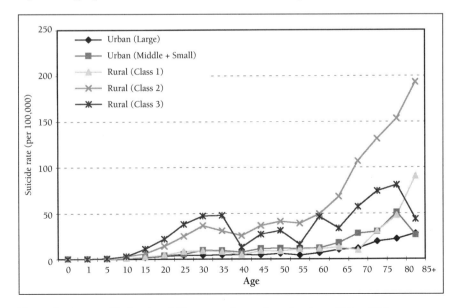

Figure 4   Age-specific female suicide rates, urban and rural regions, China, 2001.

Compared with other countries, China had a relatively lower rate of suicide in large urban regions, and the suicide rates in medium and small urban regions were similar to that of the large urban regions. However, in areas of lower economic standing, such as Class 2 and Class 3 rural regions, the suicide rates were significantly higher when compared with the suicide rates of other countries. In 2001, suicide rates in large, medium and small urban regions, and Class 1, Class 2, and Class 3 rural regions were 5.14, 7.06, 8.29, 23.71, and 19.47 per 100,000, respectively. Suicide rates in the Class 1 rural areas were similar to the urban suicide rates. Interestingly, it was Class 2 rural areas, rather than Class 3, that had the highest suicide rates in most age groups. Hence, the national suicide rate of China is a composite of the relatively low urban suicide rates and the high suicide rates in both Class 2 and Class 3 rural regions.

In some Western countries, such as Canada, the USA, Australia, and the UK, suicide rates for the elderly were slightly higher than the average population. In some European countries, such as Germany and Austria, suicide rates for the elderly were almost three times higher than the average suicide rate for the population. In China, the difference between suicide rates in the elderly and in the average population was even more significant, especially in males. This is clearly demonstrated in Table 3, which shows the ratio of age-specific suicide rates to that of the total population. When compared with the overall suicide rate, the ratios for the groups below 65 years of age were less than 2, and the ratios for the groups aged 65 years and above were more than 2 in the urban areas. The similar cut-off point in rural areas was 60. In the group aged 75 years and above, the same ratio was between 3 and 10 for both males and females.

Gender Ratio of Suicide

Of all the countries that supply suicide rates to the WHO, China is the only country where females have a higher suicide rate than males. We can see from Table 1 that the ratios of male and female suicide rates in Western countries were 3 or above. Although the suicide rates for Asian countries are comparatively lower than their Western counterparts, the male suicide rates are still generally higher than the female suicide rates. For example, in Japan, Singapore, Hong Kong, and Taiwan, the gender ratio of suicide rates were 1.9, 1.5, 1.3, and 1.9, respectively.

However, since the female suicide rates in China have decreased significantly more quickly than male suicides in the 1990s, the gender ratio of suicide changed accordingly in the same period. Figure 5 shows the male-female ratio of suicide in rural and urban areas: the male-female ratio of suicide in urban areas gradually increased between 1991 and 2001, and the ratio had exceeded 1 in 1999. The

Table 2. Age- and Gender-Specific Suicide Rates, Urban and Rural Regions, China, 2001.

Age	Urban regions		Rural regions		
	Large	Medium/ small	Class 1	Class 2	Class 3
Male					
15–9	1.17	0.61	2.64	4.39	7.07
20–4	2.63	4.65	4.55	8.86	9.79
25–9	3.81	4.62	5.34	14.59	18.18
30–4	5.11	8.71	7.20	21.99	25.39
35–9	6.69	7.13	10.30	27.15	18.65
40–4	7.56	8.30	8.69	24.76	20.89
45–9	8.27	10.34	11.30	33.68	27.33
50–4	6.96	11.51	14.90	37.33	28.58
55–9	6.54	6.95	10.30	38.72	22.02
60–4	7.36	12.67	26.46	68.01	39.07
65–9	8.86	25.42	32.60	81.08	64.54
70–4	11.39	27.56	28.22	122.65	95.37
75–9	20.55	35.68	39.22	146.48	116.63
80–4	36.87	63.57	69.89	199.53	68.18
85+	39.04	28.09	93.06	167.92	24.06
Total	5.48	6.77	9.26	22.22	16.72
Female					
15–9	1.79	2.31	2.43	5.89	11.03
20–4	3.33	4.03	4.57	14.09	21.95
25–9	4.30	5.26	8.45	24.82	38.24
30–4	4.33	9.60	9.04	36.54	47.12
35–9	4.36	9.40	8.14	30.98	47.78
40–4	4.92	7.41	4.80	25.64	13.04
45–9	4.51	11.42	9.09	36.60	27.06
50–4	6.14	11.79	8.69	41.09	31.16
55–9	4.10	11.27	10.76	39.06	15.94
60–4	6.73	12.04	11.17	49.36	46.20
65–9	10.08	17.66	12.82	68.17	33.77
70–4	11.60	28.02	9.62	106.96	57.01
75–9	19.25	30.11	30.75	131.37	74.10
80–4	22.05	50.88	47.69	153.31	80.80
85+	27.85	26.04	90.45	193.20	43.62
Total	4.78	7.36	7.32	25.29	22.50

male-female ratio of suicide in rural areas fluctuated in the same period and had been increasing since 1995, but remained under 1 in 2001.

Yip and Liu (2006) have pointed out the ecological fallacy in thinking that what is true at the group level must be true at the individual level. Applied to the issue of gender ratio for suicide in China, one simple explanation of different suicide rates between nations, as stated in Moksony's composition theory, is that the national populations differ in the proportion of those at risk for suicide. There

Table 3. Ratio of Suicide Rates Between Age Groups and the Total Population in
Five Different Regions, China, 2001.

Age	Urban regions		Rural regions		
	Large cities	Medium/ small cities	Class 1 regions	Class 2 regions	Class 3 regions
Males					
15-19	0.21	0.09	0.29	0.20	0.42
20-24	0.48	0.69	0.49	0.40	0.59
25-29	0.70	0.68	0.58	0.66	1.09
30-34	0.93	1.29	0.78	0.99	1.52
35-39	1.22	1.05	1.11	1.22	1.12
40-45	1.38	1.23	0.94	1.11	1.25
45-49	1.51	1.53	1.22	1.52	1.63
50-54	1.27	1.70	1.61	1.68	1.71
55-59	1.19	1.03	1.11	1.74	1.32
60-64	1.34	1.87	2.86	3.06	2.34
65-69	1.62	3.75	3.52	3.65	3.86
70-74	2.08	4.07	3.05	5.52	5.70
75-79	3.75	5.27	4.24	6.59	6.98
80-84	6.73	9.39	7.55	8.98	4.08
85+	7.12	4.15	10.05	7.56	1.44
Females					
15-19	0.33	0.34	0.26	0.27	0.66
20-24	0.61	0.60	0.49	0.63	1.31
25-29	0.78	0.78	0.91	1.12	2.29
30-34	0.79	1.42	0.98	1.64	2.82
35-39	0.80	1.39	0.88	1.39	2.86
40-45	0.90	1.09	0.52	1.15	0.78
45-49	0.82	1.69	0.98	1.65	1.62
50-54	1.12	1.74	0.94	1.85	1.86
55-59	0.75	1.66	1.16	1.76	0.95
60-64	1.23	1.78	1.21	2.22	2.76
65-69	1.84	2.61	1.38	3.07	2.02
70-74	2.12	4.14	1.04	4.81	3.41
75-79	3.51	4.45	3.32	5.91	4.43
80-84	4.02	7.52	5.15	6.90	4.83
85+	5.08	3.85	9.77	8.69	2.61

is a large age difference in the age- and gender-specific suicide rates in China
(Figure 6). In urban regions, females under the age of 30 had a higher suicide
rate than their male counterparts, which made the ratio of male to female suicide
rates less than 1; however, the suicide rates of males over age 30 were higher than
females. In rural regions, there was a close relationship between suicide rates and
age group, and the ratio of male to female suicide rate increased with age. Females
under the age of 40 had a higher suicide rate than males, with a male to female

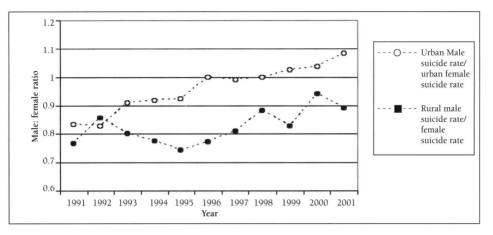

Figure 5   Male-female ratio of suicide, rural and urban regions, China, 1991–2001.

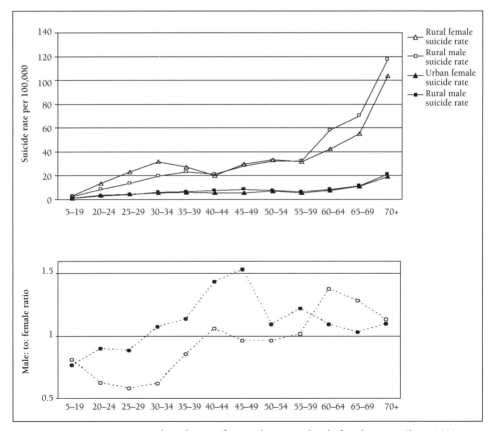

Figure 6   Region-, age-, and gender-specific suicide rates and male-female ratios, China, 2001.

Note: Adapted from Yip P. S. F. and K. Y. Liu. (2006). The ecological fallacy of gender ratio of suicide in China. British Journal of Psychiatry. 189: 465–466.

ratio of less than 1; males 60 years and above had a higher suicide rate than females in the same age group, with a male to female ratio greater than 1. Although China's gender ratio for suicide was still less than 1 in 2001, closer examination revealed that it was mostly driven by the high suicide rate in one particular population sub-group, namely, the young women aged 25–34 in rural China.

Marital Status and Suicide

As noted by Durkheim (1897[1951]) a century ago, suicide rates differ according to marital status. This pattern also has been found in Asian countries (Yip 1998). Because the MOH system does not require cities to report martial status, the analysis below was based on data collected from Shanghai districts. Shanghai provides one of the largest sample populations for the MOH death registration system, and the quality of the death registration system is among the best within the country.

Table 4 shows suicide rates by age, gender, and marital status from 1992 to 1995 from Shanghai districts. For both males and females, those who were married had the lowest suicide rates, and those who were widowed had the highest suicide rates. Suicide rates of single and divorced people fell between the two. For males aged 15 and above, the suicide rates for married, single, divorced, and widowed were 4.8, 5.4, 19.0, and 25.7 per 100,000, respectively. The corresponding figures for females were 4.5, 4.7, 9.9, and 18.3 per 100,000, respectively. This pattern was consistent across all age groups. Despite the small sample size, the suicide rate among those males aged 15–9 and married was very high.

Table 4. Suicide Rates by Age, Gender, and Martial Status, Shanghai, 1992–95.

Age	Single	Married	Widowed	Divorced
Male				
15–19	2.7	115.8	0.0	0.0
20–29	4.6	3.1	0.0	4.6
30–39	9.8	3.9	11.3	19.3
40–49	7.8	2.9	34.0	19.5
50–59	15.4	5.0	15.8	18.8
60+	31.3	8.6	26.1	20.0
Total	5.4	4.8	25.7	19.0
Female				
15–19	3.2	0.0	0.0	0.0
20–29	5.4	5.9	61.9	30.8
30–39	8.3	3.2	25.4	7.5
40–49	6.6	2.8	12.6	6.5
50–59	14.9	5.7	19.6	4.0
60+	25.2	7.7	18.4	28.8
Total	4.7	4.5	18.3	9.9

In order to test the hypothesis that marriage is a protective factor, we used Durkhiem's Coefficient of Preservation of married persons (CP) to further analyze the relationship between marital status and suicide (Durkheim 1897[1951]; Yip 1998; Yip and Thorburn 2004). The results are shown in Table 5. The coefficients represent the suicide ratio between those who are single, divorced, and widowed against those who are married.

Generally speaking, marriage was shown to be a protective factor against suicide. The CP between widowed and married males (age 15 and above) was 5.4, and the CP between married and divorced males was 4.0. Widowed and married females (age 15 and above) had a CP of 4.1, and the CP between the divorced and the married group was 2.2. The protective effect of marriage was found across all age groups. Secondly, marriage was more of a protective factor for men than for women. The particularly high suicide risk of men divorced and widowed has contributed to the high male to female ratio in the elderly. The CPs for men widowed, divorced, and single (aged 15 or above) were all higher than that of females. However, the relative "advantage" of marriage for men varied across the age groups. Lastly, for most age groups, especially for the elderly, suicide rates for the single group were still higher than suicide rates for the married group, although the suicide rates between the single and divorced groups were not significantly different.

Table 5. Coefficient of Preservation of Married Persons by Gender, Age, and Marital Status, Shanghai, 1992–95.

Age	Single : Married		Widowed : Married		Divorced : Married	
	CP	95% CI	CP	95% CI	CP	95% CI
Male						
15–9	0.023	0.003–0.170	0.000	NA	0.000	NA
20–9	1.484	0.935–2.355	0.000	NA	1.484	0.202–11.083
30–9	2.513	1.908–3.309	2.897	0.406–20.698	4.949	1.314–5.038
40–9	2.690	1.624–4.454	11.724	5.971–23.021	6.724	1.403–6.413
50–9	3.080	1.348–7.038	3.160	1.161–8.603	3.760	0.655–33.731
60+	3.640	1.875–7.064	3.035	2.457–3.749	2.326	0.380–1.268
Total	1.125	0.969–1.307	5.354	4.454–6.437	3.958	1.387–2.914
Female						
15–9	NA	NA	NA	NA	NA	NA
20–9	0.915	0.660–1.270	10.492	1.467–75.365	5.220	1.284–21.223
30–9	2.594	1.215–5.537	7.938	2.531–24.898	2.344	1.036–5.303
40–9	2.357	0.964–5.762	4.500	2.102–9.634	2.321	0.739–7.296
50–9	2.614	0.645–10.595	3.439	2.107–5.611	0.702	0.098–5.030
60+	3.273	1.618–6.620	2.390	2.019–2.829	3.740	1.664–8.409
Total	1.044	0.864–1.263	4.067	3.573–4.629	2.200	1.378–3.513

CP=coefficient of Preservation of married persons; 95%CI =95% confidence interval of CP.

Suicide Methods

Table 6 shows the different methods of suicide in Shanghai from the years 1992 to 1996. The ratio of the number of male suicides to the number of female suicides is 0.95 in this sample. Results from the table show that the two most common methods were poisoning and hanging, each making up about 36% of all suicide deaths. Jumping from a height constituted around 16%. There was a certain discrepancy between the suicide methods that males and females chose. The most common method of suicide among men was hanging (38.8%), followed by poisoning (29.8%). For women, poisoning was the most commonly used method (43.8%), although a substantial number of female suicides were also by hanging (33.5%).

Table 6. Methods of Suicide, Shanghai, 1992–96.

Method	Male		Female		Overall	
	N	%	N	%	N	%
Poisoning	418	29.75	648	43.84	1,066	36.98
Hanging	545	38.79	495	33.49	1,040	36.07
Jumping from a height	262	18.65	198	13.40	460	15.96
Others	180	12.81	137	9.27	317	11.00
Total	1,405	100.00	1,478	100.00	2,883	100.00

Discussion

A number of important questions have been raised about the epidemiology of suicide in China: Why is the suicide rate in China higher than that of many other countries? Why is the female suicide rate high, especially in rural China? Why is there such a large rural and urban difference in suicide rates? Following is a brief discussion on these important questions that should continue to receive much research attention.

High National Suicide Rate

The high suicide rate in China may reflect some cultural aspects of China. Firstly, Buddhism, Confucianism, and Taoism have great influence on the Chinese culture. These religious/moral traditions arguably have a more permissive attitude towards suicide than the Western tradition. For example, in Buddhist teachings, spirit never dies, and death of the body is an escape from the "corrupt" world. But it should be noted that, although it may not be considered as sinful in Buddhism as in Christianity, death from suicide does not lead to nirvana and only means further suffering after reincarnation.

Secondly, one may argue that there is a connection between suicide and the "Chinese personality" and social relationships. Traditionally, feelings are often expressed subtly. Lack of avenues to express one's emotion may contribute to interpersonal difficulties and suicidal risk. In addition, social interactions in Chinese society are often limited to family or blood relatives, which can be detrimental when family disputes occur. This is especially true for rural women who do not necessarily have a very good social network and support system. Also, high expectation for one to conform to social responsibility may lead to unrealistic expectations towards others as well as to self. However, as Table 1 indicates, the suicide rates in Hong Kong, Taiwan, and Singapore were relatively low, and the suicide rates in China's urban regions were also relatively low. It may be a too simplistic view that associates a high suicide rate with Chinese culture.

A third potential explanation of the high suicide rate in China lies in the epidemiology of mental disorders. Cheng (1995) studied in Taiwan and stated that 97% of people who died from suicide deaths were depressed or had abused drug and alcohol. Although there is a lack of reliable epidemiological data on the prevalence of mental disorders in China, it is unlikely that the prevalence will be twice that of Western countries and will fully explain the differences in the suicide rates. Moreover, alcohol and drug use is still relatively uncommon in China.

Finally, another explanation may be the economic hardship faced by many people living in China, especially in rural China (Yip et al. 2005). The discrepancy of urban and rural suicide rates lend some support to this view. However, it is well known that there is no simple relationship between economic development and suicide rates. For instance, other Asian countries with similar or lower levels of economic development have lower suicide rates than in China. For example, the Philippines had a very low suicide rate, and, apparently, the mental well-being of Pilipinos is much better than other Asian neighbors. In contrast, Japan, with the highest GDP per capita in the Asia region, has the highest suicide rate.

The discussion above has outlined the difficulty of having a single explanation for the high suicide rates in China. Phillips and colleagues (1999) propose five interacting and mutually dependent factors that lead to a high suicide rate in China. They include (1) cultural beliefs in the afterlife and acceptance of suicide as a solution of personal problems; (2) prevalence of social problems; (3) contributions from psychological problems such as depression; (4) availability of lethal means (i.e., pesticides and rat poisons); and (5) lack of suicide prevention services.

High Female Suicide Rates

Cultural reasons also have been proposed to explain the high female suicide rates in China. Firstly, it has been suggested that the pressure that Chinese traditions put on women results in an introverted and masochistic personality, which, in turn, affects their ability to cope with stress and high suicide risk.

Secondly, Chinese women are traditionally dependent on their husband and family, and they lack external social and financial support. Thus, in a close-knit Chinese family, the slightest dispute may result in a suicide (Pearson and Liu 2002; Pearson et al. 2002). This is related to the low social status of women, although women's social status has greatly improved in recent decades.

Thirdly, it has been suggested that the high female suicide rates in China are mainly driven by the high lethality of the method used in rural areas (Phillips et al. 2002). Like women in other countries, poisoning is the most commonly used method. However, with the wide availability of pesticides and rat poisons in rural China, the mortality of the attempts is very high compared to those from industrial countries, where drugs typically involved are much less lethal (e.g., pain killers). While we believe that the high lethality of suicide attempts that use pesticide and rat poisons certainly have contributed to the high female suicide rates in China, the relatively lower male-female ratios in urban China, Hong Kong, and Taiwan suggest there may be other factors.

High Rural Suicide Rates

As mentioned above, the economic hardship of the rural communities may be one of the reasons why rural suicide rates are high in China (Yip et al. 2005). It may also explain our results which show that affluent rural areas (Class 1) have similar suicide rates as urban regions. But it is unclear whether the associated social changes (e.g., in family structure, educational opportunity, health care system, and economic activities) also have contributed to their low suicide rates. In contrast, the less economically developed rural areas may have still preserved the traditional family relations. Given a more kinship-oriented social organization, interpersonal conflicts and family disputes may occur more frequently in rural than in urban areas (and the wealthy rural areas) and have a greater impact on those who are distressed. Economic hardship in the face of great economic disparities may also have triggered more interpersonal conflicts in rural families. The problems arising from the economic disparity may explain why the sufficient rural areas (Class 2) have higher suicide rates than the most deprived areas (Class 3).

Suicide is among the leading causes of death. The economic loss due to suicide is substantial. In terms of years of life lost, suicide has caused China dearly (Yip et al. 2005). Much research attention has been given to explain the high suicide rates in China, but less is known about the low urban suicide rates. It may be due to the economic advantage enjoyed by urban dwellers, especially in large cities. Further research should be conducted on the protective factors enjoyed by the urban population in China.

Suicide Prevention in China

One of the biggest challenges of suicide prevention is the lack of empirical evidence of what constitutes effective prevention. Evaluative studies of suicide prevention programs in China are close to nonexistent. Specific prevention efforts have to be tailor-made according to the country's pattern of suicide, as reflected by accurate monitoring and analysis of the mortality data. The WHO suggest the "six steps" for suicide prevention, which included the treatment of psychiatric patients; guns possession control; detoxification of domestic gas; and toning down reports in the press (WHO 1998). Limiting accessibility of lethal methods, which in China is pesticides and rat poisoning, has been suggested as a cost-effective method of reducing suicide in rural area, especially among women. It is expected to produce some immediate effect.

For medium and long-term prevention effort, it has been shown that rural women tend to suffer more from poor education, limited job opportunities, and poverty in rural China. Significant economic development has been observed in China in the past decade, however, the difference in wealth between the rural and urban area is still of great concern. We speculate that the decrease in the suicide rates among young rural women might be due to the newly emerged employment and education opportunities, especially in the cities. It might serve as a means of escape for young rural women in distress. The rural women aged between 20 and 39 are more likely to be married and might not have benefited as much from the social changes. A study of suicide attempts among young rural women showed that over half of the precipitating events prior to the suicide attempts were related to an unhappy marriage (Pearson et al. 2002) Moreover, qualitative studies demonstrated that suicide might serve as a means of rebellion among young, married, rural women in light of their low status within the family system (Pearson and Liu 2002). Further research is needed to investigate the roles of poor family relationship and domestic violence in shaping the pattern of suicide among rural women in China, as well as the potential benefit of family education programs.

Based on the previous successful experience of suicide prevention (Knox et al. 2003), community-wide suicide prevention programs aimed at decreasing stigma, enhancing social networks, facilitating help-seeking behavior, etc., might be of value in helping some of the rural women, although their effectiveness needs to be evaluated. Most importantly, the Chinese government should realize the consequence of the social and economic loss of suicides, especially among those who are economically active. We call for setting up prevention programs for this group. Improvement in the general welfare, employment conditions, and health-care services are expected to produce a positive impact on reducing the number of suicides, especially in rural China.

In summary, much still needs to be learned about the relationship between suicide rates and factors such as economic development, distribution of wealth, health care system, social status of women, family relationships, mental health of rural and urban populations, and other culturally specific factors. Much will be gained from studies that combine macro-socioeconomic and epidemiological data with individual level data, as well as comparative research on the widely diverse communities in China.

5

Hong Kong

C. K. Law and Paul S. F. Yip

The suicide rate in Hong Kong remained stable up until the mid-1990s. Since then, it has increased significantly. This study aims to examine changes in the Hong Kong suicide rate over the period 1993–2003 and discuss possible impacts on the community. It is a retrospective study based on the registered death files of suicide deaths in Hong Kong. In 2003, Hong Kong showed a 25% increase in suicide rates since 1997, with a rate of 18.6 per 100,000, which is a historical high. This increasing trend is worrying. In 2003, suicide ranked as the sixth leading cause of death and represented about 3% of all deaths. The proportion of Years of Life Lost (YLL) due to suicides was 8.1% in 2003. This increase can mainly be attributed to an increase in the suicide rate among those aged 25–59. Since the mid-1990s, there has emerged a new method of carbon monoxide poisoning by charcoal burning that became the second most commonly used method of suicide by 2001. The use of charcoal burning increased from 2% in 1998 to about 26% in 2003. Death by charcoal burning has not simply displaced older methods, but it also seems to draw from an enlarged at-risk population. The increase in suicides has had a significant adverse effect on the economic and health performance in Hong Kong. It has been suggested that most of the increase is related to the unfavorable economic environment, poor mental health, disintegration of family support, and disconnection within the community (Liu et al. 2007; Yip et al. 2003).

Introduction

Situated on the southeastern edge of Guangdong Province in China, Hong Kong has been a Special Administrative Region (SAR) of the People's Republic of China (PRC) since 1997. It has a land area of 1,103 km² and is made up of Hong Kong Island, Kowloon and the New Territories, and 262 outlying islands. Since 1842, the territory had been a British dependent territory, before its sovereignty was returned to the PRC in 1997. Economically, Hong Kong is one of the most significant international cities and business centers in the western Pacific region. According to the latest figures made available from the World Development Indicators (WDI) of the World Bank (2004), Hong Kong has become the second wealthiest and most economically productive place, excluding Japan, throughout the entire region. By 2002, per capita gross national income (GNI) here had reached US$24,690, which was almost 25 times higher than the figure for China and 20% higher than that of Singapore, its main economic competitor in the region.

This economic prosperity has brought about a rising standard of living and health care. Life expectancy in Hong Kong is one of the highest in the world. Life expectancy at birth for Hong Kong residents increased from 72.3 years in 1981 to 78.5 in 2003 for males, and from 78.5 to 84.4 for females. However, to seek further improvement in health performance, suicide should not be ignored, as this has become a prominent public health issue in Hong Kong (Yip et al. 2003; WHO 2002). From the early 1980s, the territory-wide annual suicide rate had remained at a stable level of around 12 per 100,000. However, the annual number of suicides increased by 61% from 784 in 1997 to 1,264 in 2003, which accounted for about 3% of total deaths in the year.

In this chapter, we study the changes in the profiles of completed suicides in Hong Kong and explore the association of suicide rates with changes in the socioeconomic environment over the period 1993–2003. The number of divorces increased sixfold from 2,000 cases in 1990 to 12,000 cases in 2003. The proportion that never married also increased from 5% to more than 20%. The traditional role of the family in the community is less prominent than previously. In addition, the occurrence of the Asian economic turmoil in November 1997 seriously affected the economic climate in Hong Kong. The Severe Acute Respiratory Syndrome (SARS) epidemic, in mid-2003, drove Hong Kong into stagnation (with a historically high unemployment rate of 7.8%). We also study the impact of changes in method, especially the rising popularity of charcoal burning, on the overall risk for suicide. A comparison of suicide and other leading causes of death is carried out, highlighting the significance of suicide prevention to population health improvements in the Hong Kong community.

Data and Methods

Suicide data for the period 1990–2003 were obtained from the registered death files through the Census and Statistics Department of Hong Kong (C&SD, 1990–2004). Hong Kong has a well-developed death reporting system to record all deaths and related information on the deceased. The coverage rate of the data is almost complete, with very good data quality. At present, all unnatural deaths in Hong Kong are presented to the Coroner's Court to determine the underlying cause of death. The coronial system in Hong Kong is very similar to the British system: the coroner has to be satisfied beyond reasonable doubt that the death was self-inflicted and that there was an intention to die (Coroner Court 2005). For the period 1990–2000, suicide deaths were defined as those where the external cause code ranged from E950 to E959, according to the International Classification of Diseases, Ninth Revision (ICD-9) (WHO 1978). For the year 2001 onward, the schema of the International Statistical Classification of Diseases and Related Health Problems, Tenth Revision (ICD-10) was used. Suicides were identified as those where the external code ranged from X60 to X84 (WHO 1992).

To study the transition trend of suicide rates, three forms of death rate were used: crude suicide death rates (CSDR), standardized suicide mortality rates through direct standardization (SSMR), and age-specific suicide mortality rates (ASMR).

Also, suicide rates by marital status and occupation over the period were separately assessed. In an earlier work, family and social support was identified as one of the most prominent protective factors for suicidal behavior (CSRP 2005). Subject to social isolation, ex-married and non-working people have been considered as having a higher suicide risk. Here, we verify that argument by examining the risk ratios for these two factors and comparing the post-1997 rates with the pre-1997 figures to assess whether any significant pattern changes have occurred. The suicide rates for the employed group were further categorized into three subgroups[1] based on the occupational classification of the International Labor Office (1990). The distribution of suicide methods used was assessed to identify whether any pattern changes in method have occurred since the first charcoal burning suicide case was reported in late 1998 (Chan et al. 2005).

Finally, the socioeconomic burden related to premature death by suicide was assessed and compared with other leading causes of death in Hong Kong, using the YLL approach, a standardized measure for disease burden proposed in the Global Burden of Disease (GBD) project of the World Health Organization (Murray 1996); we use this to estimate how many adjusted life years have been lost due to suicide over the past few decades.

---

1. High income group: Professional, administrative & executive; Medium income group: Clerical, sales & services; Low income group: Production & elementary occupations.

Results

Increase in the Suicide Rate

Between 1990 and 2003, the annual number of suicide deaths in Hong Kong increased by 73.4%, from 729 to 1,264, while the corresponding figures for all deaths only increased by 26.9%, from 29,136 to 36,971, for the same period. Suicide constituted 3.4% of all deaths in 2003 and was one of the most prominent causes of death for the non-elderly (below 60) in Hong Kong (13.4%). Figure 1 gives the crude and standardized suicide rates for 1990–2003, which confirm the difference in suicide rate transition before and after 1997. From 1990 to 1996, the crude suicide rate of Hong Kong remained at a fairly stable level of around 13 per 100,000. However, older adults have a higher suicide rate in Hong Kong. By adjusting the overall demographic change through direct standardization, it was found that the standardized suicide rate had actually followed a downward trend from 12.8 to a low of 10.6 in 1996. This downward trend then ceased, and the standardized rate increased back to the base year level in 2000. By 2003, the SSMR reached 17 (the crude rate was 18.6), which was 32.8% higher than the 1990 level. Part of the increase between 1990 and 2003 was due to an aging population, but a more significant reason is the drastic increase in the suicide rate across age groups over the period.

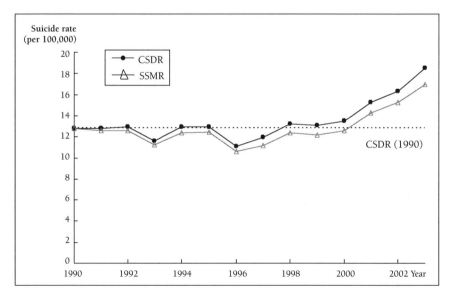

Figure 1   Crude suicide death rate (CSDR) and standardized suicide mortality rate (SSMR) in Hong Kong, 1990–2003.

Figure 2 gives the age-specific suicide rates for 1990–2003. As noted, older adults (aged 60+) had the highest suicide rate. It also highlights that the suicide rate for young adults (25–39) has undergone a significant increase from 14 in 1990 to 19.4 in 2003, and, for the middle aged (40–59), the rate has increased by more than 60%, from 13.4 to 21.5 for the same period.

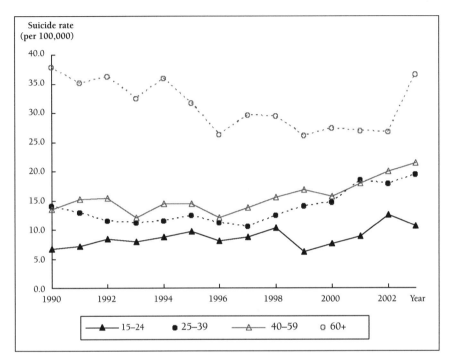

Figure 2   Age-specific suicide rates in Hong Kong, 1990–2003.

Marital Status

Table 1 gives the age-, sex-, and marital-status-specific suicide rates in Hong Kong for the periods 1991–96 and 1997–2003. On average, the now-married group (aged 25 or above) had a lower suicide risk compared with other groups for the same period.

This table suggests that the protective effect of marriage has been more significant for males than for females since 1997. Suicide rates for the never married and the ex-married groups (divorced or widowed) were comparatively higher than the baseline (now married) in the same respective age and sex groups from 1991 to 2003. The relative risk for never married persons below 60 has been comparatively stable over the period, while the risk ratio for ex-married men aged 25–59 has increased drastically from below 2 in the period 1991–96 to

Table 1. Age-, Sex-, and Marital-Status-Specific Suicide Rates (per 100,000)
in Hong Kong, 1991–96 and 1997–2003.

Age group	Marital status	Male		Female	
		1991–96	1997–2003	1991–96	1997–2003
15–24	Never married	8.5	10.8	5.4	6.4
	Married	9.9	23.6	9.1	9.3
	Ex-married	–	–	–	–
25–39	Never married	18.2	29.7	10.8	12.5
	Married	7	10.5	5.7	7
	Ex-married	15.2	187.6	9.3	38
40–59	Never married	49.1	69.7	15.6	18.6
	Married	9.4	14.9	9	9.4
	Ex-married	16.9	130.3	4.7	17.9
60+	Never married	70.1	79.7	25.5	17.9
	Married	29.6	29.4	40.1	26.8
	Ex-married	11.6	35.5	8.5	4.8

10.7 in the period 1997–2003. It should also be noted that the corresponding figures for ex-married females showed a significant, but less prominent, increase from about 0.8 to 2.7 over this period. This suggests that men in Hong Kong are better "protected" by marriage, and the increasing suicide risk for ex-married men should be of great concern when setting out local suicide prevention strategies in the future.

Occupation

Table 2 presents the suicide rates for those aged 15–59, by sex and occupation, for the two separate periods 1990–94 and 1999–2003, respectively. Overall, the suicide risk for employed persons was around 50% lower than the overall rate. No major difference between genders was observed across the period.

Table 2. Sex- and Occupation-Specific Suicide Rates (per 100,000)
in Hong Kong, 1990–94 and 1999–2003.

Type of occupation		1990–94		1999–2003	
		Suicide cases (N)	Rate	Suicide cases (N)	Rate
High	M	55	2.31	278	8.48
	F	23	2.25	109	6.13
Middle	M	230	10.93	212	10.58
	F	110	4.47	156	5.00
Low	M	233	5.50	420	11.02
	F	38	2.26	89	4.38
Working group	M	518	5.94	910	10.00
	F	153	2.97	354	5.11
Overall (15–59)	M	1381	13.90	2432	21.80
	F	900	9.57	1246	10.49

Given the rapid increase in the suicide rate among the employed, this table suggests that, after the period 1990–94, the protective effect of employment was probably reduced, if not removed. Table 2 shows that the suicide rate for employed males increased by 68%, from around 6 per 100,000 in 1990–94 to around 10.0 in 1999–2003, while the figures for all working age males display an even more dramatic increase of 72%, from 3 to 5.1 over the same period. Nevertheless, employed persons still had a lower suicide rate, when compared with the general population in the same respective ages, at 21.8 for males and 10.5 for females, for the period 1999–2003.

Further analysis of the suicide statistics within the working group reveals that the high-risk group for suicide shifted from mid-income workers to a bimodal pattern. The increase in the suicide rate for the male high-income group has been the most prominent, increasing by almost 300% from only around 2 in 1990–94 to 8 in 1999–2003, and for women from 2.3 to 6.1. On the other hand, the low-income group remained the group at greatest risk for the period 1999–2003, and it also showed a significant increase of around 100%, for males from 5.5 to 11.0, and for females from 3.0 to 5.1, when compared with the 1990–94 figures. Finally, the mid-income group showed the most stable pattern, with a rate maintained at around 11 for males and 5 for females over the same period.

Increase in Years of Life Lost

For the period 1990–2003, the relative ranking of suicide death in all deaths went up gradually from ninth in 1990 to eighth in 1997, and to sixth in 2003. The increase in ranking in terms of the burden of suicide was, however, even more significant. Suicide has become one of the most prominent causes of YLL in Hong Kong. Figure 3 shows the number and proportion of YLL attributed to suicide in Hong Kong from 1990 to 2003. The total number of YLL for suicide deaths increased by 72%, from about 13,500 years (5.0%) in 1990 to 23,300 years (8.8%) in 2003. On the other hand, the total YLL for all causes of death decreased by 2%, from 269,800 years to 264,800 years over the same period, due to a reduction in mortality. Consequently, the ranking of suicide in terms of YLL increased from fourth in 1990 to third in 2003.

Change of Method Used

The pattern of suicide methods changed over the period. One of the most striking features was the increase in charcoal burning, as shown in Figure 4 and Table 3. The proportion of suicide by charcoal burning increased from 2% in 1998 to

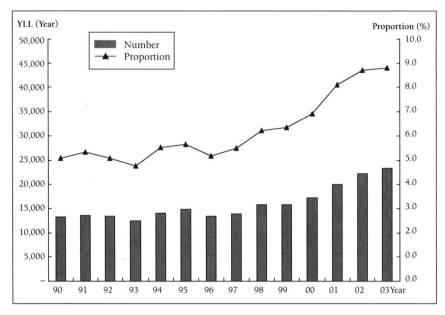

Figure 3   Number and proportion of years of life lost (YLL) attributed to suicide in Hong Kong, 1990–2003.

more than a quarter of total suicide deaths in 2003, replacing hanging as the second most commonly used method for suicide. Although jumping remained the most commonly used method, due to its accessibility and lethality (Lo & Leung 1985; Yip 1996; 1997), and accounting for 46% of the total suicides in 2003, the rising popularity of charcoal burning is of great concern. Commonly perceived as a comfortable, nonviolent, and non-disfiguring way to end one's life, it is of great concern that charcoal burning may draw in people who would not otherwise consider suicide. Our earlier studies (Chan et al. 2005) found that people who committed suicide using charcoal burning did not have the typical profile of suicide victims (i.e., unemployed, of older age, and with mental illness). Furthermore, there has been no sign to indicate that the growth of charcoal burning suicides in Hong Kong has caused any reduction in suicides by other methods, suggesting that this new method has generated a new cohort of suicide completers.

Table 3. Suicides in Hong Kong by Method Used, 1990–2003.

Year	Method				
	Hanging	Jumping	Poisoning	Charcoal burning	Others
1990	204	409	56	0	60
1991	220	432	36	0	47
1992	228	404	59	0	58
1993	215	383	42	0	44
1994	221	454	47	0	58
1995	222	464	60	0	53
1996	223	385	67	0	47
1997	240	453	46	1	44
1998	287	442	56	16	66
1999	231	383	53	145	56
2000	232	392	49	176	53
2001	219	454	38	253	55
2002	255	480	42	276	56
2003	246	584	51	321	62

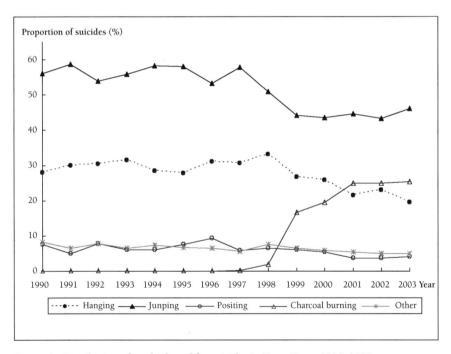

Figure 4   Distribution of method used for suicides in Hong Kong, 1990–2003.

Discussion

In the past, suicide was seldom considered a prominent public health issue in Hong Kong, since the crude suicide rate maintained a fairly stable level and was below the global average. The fact that older adults had the highest suicide rate caused some concern in the community. Most older suicide completers had suffered from a chronic disease (Yip & Chi 2001; CSRP 2005), suggesting that the existing service provision for medical and health care may not be sufficient to cater to the needs of this group. This situation will get worse due to the problem of the rapidly aging population in Hong Kong. It is estimated that 27% of the population will be aged 65 or above in 2033 (C&SD 2004). With the advent of an aging society, it is important for policymakers to have a thorough understanding of the existing situation for older adults, so that timely and efficient measures can be set out to properly rectify this potential problem in the community.

In an attempt to alleviate the negative impacts from suicide, stakeholders for suicide prevention have put considerable effort, over the past few decades, into tackling the problem of suicide among the elderly. Through collaboration among the government, frontline workers, nongovernmental organizations, and tertiary institutions, public awareness of the importance of the care of the elderly has been widely promoted in the community. These efforts have apparently contributed to the reduction in suicide in older adults since 1994. However, an increase in older adult suicide was found in 2003. More work needs to be done to understand older adult suicide (Chan et al. 2006).

However, the overall trend of suicide rates for the general population has not benefited from a reduction in the elderly suicide rate: the increase in suicide rates among young adults and middle-aged groups has offset the reduction in elderly suicide rates over the period 1990–2003. The recent increase in suicide rates among these age groups can be related to financial difficulties. Hong Kong had a high unemployment rate of 7.8% during the SARS epidemic, and this is likely to stay at more than 5% despite the recent economic recovery. The unemployed are overrepresented among suicide deaths (Coroner Court 2005). Financial debt is mainly related to unmanageable spending, impulsive gambling, or unemployment. This may be linked to the unfavorable economic environment since the Asian economic turmoil and the global economic downturn in 1998. In contrast, there is no evidence to suggest that the political change in 1997 has had any direct effect on the suicide rate. Nevertheless, the unsatisfactory governorship of the administration could make things worse, rather than having a direct effect on the suicide rate.

Jumping remains the most commonly used method in Hong Kong. This can be explained by the accessibility and lethality of the method (Lo & Leung 1985; Yip 1996; 1997) Currently, over 80% of Hong Kong people live in skyscrapers. Since its first known use in 1998 (Lee et al. 2002), charcoal burning has not only been used as a substitute, but has also stimulated a new cohort of individuals to kill themselves. Extensive press coverage of charcoal burning deaths has been suggested as a link to its popularity (Chan et al. 2003; Yip and Lee 2007). It is used among adults with financial problems. The media have played an important role in shaping the talk of a charcoal-burning epidemic. Apart from spreading the myth of an "easy death," the news media could have unnecessarily encouraged the public to use the deadly method to by over-zealous reporting and elaborate descriptions of the method (Chan et al. 2003; Takahashi 2004). Our ethnographic investigation in Hong Kong showed that suicidal individuals chose charcoal burning because they were reminded of the method by regular newspaper reports (Chan et al. 2005). The first charcoal burning suicide victim in Taiwan also explicitly stated that he had learned of the method from the website of a Hong Kong newspaper. Charcoal burning suicide is not merely a Chinese or local health issue. The method has recently been demonstrated to spread quickly in non-Chinese societies in Hong Kong. In late 2004, seven teenagers who became acquainted in an Internet chat room committed suicide by burning charcoal in a van. The suicide pact was widely reported by the local media. In the ensuing two months, six further charcoal burning suicide pacts occurred, taking a toll of 22 lives. The spread of charcoal burning from Hong Kong to Taiwan and then to Japan has thus far followed a specific pattern. The method was "transmitted" from one society to another by the Internet, and then disseminated rapidly within a society via media reports that were excessively detailed and sensational. It remains to be seen whether the method will continue to be spread to other societies and continents via the Internet-cum-media transmission route.

The decrease in total YLL for all causes over the reference period suggests that fewer deaths are occurring at young ages. It is estimated that more than 14% of the population in 2001 was more than 60 years old. In contrast, suicide deaths among adults have recently experienced a significant increase and have contributed to the significant rise in the proportion of YLL.

Suicide has increased significantly since 1998 in Hong Kong. The socioeconomic environment in previous years has been difficult, with an increase in single-parent families. Cases of battered spouses have increased by more than 100% over the period. Finally, with an aging population, the suicide rate in Hong Kong is expected to increase if there is no significant reduction in the risk factors for suicide in the foreseeable future. A comprehensive suicide prevention program is very much needed in the community.

Appendix

The formula for YLL has been generalized from a single death at age *a* to include a parameter *K* that can be used in sensitivity analysis to remove non-uniform age-weights. The general formula for computing YLL is

$$YLL = \frac{KCe^{ra}}{(r+\beta)^2} \left\{ e^{-(r+\beta)(L+a)}\left[-(r+\beta)(L+a)-1\right] - e^{-(r+\beta)a}\left[-(r+\beta)(a)-1\right] \right\} + \frac{(1-K)}{r}\left(1-e^{rL}\right)$$

where *r* is the discount rate, β is the parameter from the age-weighting function, *K* is the age-weighting modulation factor, *C* is a constant, *a* is the age of death, and *L* is the standard expectation of life at age *a*. For standard YLL used in the GBD, *r* is 0.03, b is 0.04, *K* is 1, and *C* is 0.1658 (Murray C. J. L. 1996, 1–98).

6

Taiwan

Anne Chao, C. K. Law, P. C. Li, and Paul S. F. Yip

Based on suicide records after 1983, Taiwan's lowest suicide rate (6.2 per 100,000) was in 1993, but the rate has continuously increased to the world's average of 14.1 per 100,000 in 2003 and up to 18.8 in 2005 and 19.3 in 2006. Taiwan's increasing suicide rate trend is one of the most rapid and substantial, compared with other developing economies in the western Pacific region. The varying suicide rates of gender, age, methods, marital status, and other related factors are examined based primarily on the data from 1983 to 2003. Hanging and poisoning have been the two most commonly used methods, but charcoal burning and other gas poisoning have emerged as novel means in recent years. There are significant differences in suicide rates and methods used between rural and urban areas, due to large discrepancies in many factors. Population aging has been one of the most prominent factors in association with the rate increase since 1993. Other socioeconomic, environmental, and individual risk factors are also discussed. In the past 20 years, the middle-age group, especially for urban males, had a significant increase in risk of suicide in relation to the stress arising mainly from the economic downturn around 1995. The government-funded Taiwan Suicide Prevention Center was established in December 2005. The local authority and religious groups are now working toward preventing suicide, improving mental health service quality, and organizing community support networks.

Introduction

As a major external cause of death among adolescents and young adults, suicide is one of the most significant public health issues in the world. According to the latest figures provided by the World Health Organization (WHO) (1999, 2001), the annual global toll from suicide (815,000) exceeded the total number of deaths by homicide (500,000) and war (230,000). Compared to the world average of 14.0 per 100,000, the overall suicide rate for the western Pacific region has been significantly above the global average at 19.3 per 100,000, making suicide the leading cause of injury death. In some areas of the region, suicide rates have shown a continuously increasing trend (WHO 2005).

Situated in East Asia, Taiwan comprises the main island of Taiwan (known as Formosa), the archipelagoes of Penghu, Kinmen, Matsu, and a number of small islands. Its combined area is approximately 36,000 square km (13,900 square miles) with the population size approximately 23 million in 2007 (Government Information Office [GIO] 2007). The population density is extremely high at around 630 per square kilometer and the population is urbanized. At present, the whole area is made up of two special municipalities (Taipei City and Kaohsiung City), five provincial municipalities (Keelung, Hsinchu, Taichung, Tainan, and Chiayi Cities) and 18 counties. Of those 16 counties in Taiwan and Penghu, the area is further subdivided into 29 county municipalities and 290 townships (GIO 2007).

Ethnically, the people of Taiwan consist of two groups: an indigenous minority (2%) and a Han Chinese majority composed of Holo (native Taiwanese, approximately 73%), Hakka (approximately 13%), and mainlanders (approximately 12%). Beginning in the late 1990s, a dramatic increase in marriages between Taiwanese and foreign nationals (16.7% of all marriages in 2006) has brought more immigrants to Taiwan. Children from these marriages make up 11.7% of all babies born (GIO 2007). Mandarin is the official language, yet Holo Taiwanese is also spoken by around 70% of the people. Hakka is spoken in Hakka communities, while each of Taiwan's 13 indigenous groups has its own language.

At the end of the First Sino-Japanese War in 1895, under the Treaty of Shimonoseki, Taiwan was ceded to Japan, which ruled the island for the next 50 years. After the end of the Second World War in 1945, the Japanese surrendered and relinquished the sovereignty of Taiwan to the Nanking government before the civil war of China (GIO 2007). In 1949, when the Nationalists (Kuomintang) were defeated by the Communists in mainland China, they relocated in Taiwan and declared martial law, which was in effect for 38 years. A process of democratization has begun since the lifting of martial law in 1987. Taiwan's first democratic legislative election was held in 1992 and the first direct presidential election was held in 1996. For the past four decades, rapid economic development has transformed Taiwan from an agricultural island into a dynamic economy, with rapid industrialization, urbanization, and modernization.

Chong and Cheng (1995) addressed the suicidal behavior observed in Taiwan from 1950 to 1990. Based on records after 1983, Taiwan's lowest suicide rate was 6.2 per 100,000 in 1993, but the rate has followed a continuously upward trend since then and reached the world's average of 14.1 per 100,000 in 2003. The rate in 2004 was 15.3 and reached 18.8 in 2005 (4,282 deaths) and 19.3 in 2006 (4,406 deaths) (Department of Health 1983–2006). From an epidemiological perspective, this increasing trend in Taiwan is one of the most rapid and substantial rates in comparison with other developing economies in the western Pacific region.

In view of the increasing severity of suicide problems in Taiwan, this chapter aims to present an overview of suicide in Taiwan to enhance our understanding of this issue in order to set out a timely and cost effective measure for preventing suicide in the future. We first disseminate the epidemiological profile of those having died by suicide and methods employed, using the official data for 1983–2003. We also test whether there is a significant geographical variation between the urban and rural areas due to substantial discrepancies of living standard, income inequality, financial resources, transportation links, and public facilities between the two areas.

Data and Methods

Suicide statistics for 1983–2003 were made available from the Department of Health of the Executive Yuan of Taiwan. There is a well-established coronial system to investigate and ascertain the underlying causes of every unnatural death that has occurred. All suicide cases in Taiwan must be jointly confirmed by a district attorney and a forensic specialist or a coroner to ensure the accuracy and reliability of each suicide coding (Chou et al. 2003). With permission for research purposes, individual suicide records were retrieved from the database in accordance with the external cause of death coded from E-950 to E-959 under the International Classification of Diseases, Injuries, and Causes of Death, Ninth Revision (ICD-9) (WHO 1978). Each record contains information on the suicide deceased's age, gender, residence, marital status, dates of birth and death, and method used, respectively. Although Chong and Cheng (1995) indicated that official suicide numbers might be underestimated because some suicide cases were likely to be classified as incidental deaths, the effect of this underestimation on our general trend analysis and relative comparisons have been limited or diminished in recent years.

We examine the transition trend of three main types of suicide rates in Taiwan. They included crude suicide death rates (CSDR), age standardized suicide mortality rates through direct standardization (SSMR), and age-specific suicide mortality rates (ASMR) (Yip et al. 2003). The corresponding population statistics were used to compute suicide rates among each specified subgroup. The data were obtained from the Census Office of the Executive Yuan of Taiwan through the household registration and the household/population census. According to the provisions of laws and regulations, the registered population refers to all of the nationals maintaining household registration in Taiwan. Thus, the figure obtained should fully cover the true population size of legal residents over the period.

To test and assess the heterogeneity across the regions, we adopted Tzeng and Wu's (1986) urban-rural classification and assigned 55 municipalities and townships in Taiwan with an urbanization level of 4 or above as urban areas, and the remaining 261 districts were classified as rural areas. The two counties (Kinmen and Lienchiang) in Fuchien were not included because their urbanization level was not classifiable under the Tzeng and Wu (1986) assignment.

Results

Suicide Rates in the Taiwan over the Past 20 years

Figure 1 shows the overall and gender-specific suicide rate of Taiwan for 1983–2003. During the first ten-year period (1983–93), the overall suicide rate had shown a continuously downward trend, with a rate reduction of more than 46% from around 12.0 per 100,000 in 1983 to the lowest level of 6.2 in 1993. When comparing suicide rates between male and female, the overall rate reduction during the 1980s was mainly from females, with the rate reduced by more than 51%, from 9.4 to 4.6. The corresponding rate reduction for males was comparatively less dramatic at 44%, from 14.4 to 8.1. However, beginning in 1994, the overall rate gradually reverted upward and returned to the base year level in 2001. By 2003, the rate was further increased to 14.1 per 100,000.

Similar to other places in the world, the rate increase in Taiwan for the subsequent ten-year period (1993–2003) was attributed to the rate change among males. Since 1993, the male suicide rate increased by 130% from the lowest at 8.1 to 18.7 in 2003, while the female rate only returned to the 1983 level. As a consequence, the suicidal risk ratio for male to female widened from 1.52 to 2.00 for the period.

Figure 2 shows the age-specific suicide rate in Taiwan for 1983–2003. Generally speaking, the rate of suicide increased with age over the period. When comparing different age groups over the past 20 years, we note the rate for adolescents and young adults below 30 years of age has remained at a stable level

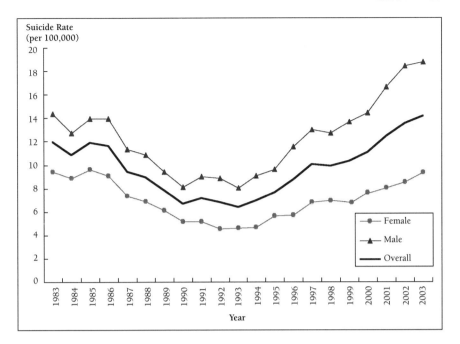

Figure 1 Suicide rates by gender in Taiwan, 1983–2003.

over the period, indicating that any changes in the overall suicide rate corresponded almost entirely to the higher age groups. Detailed age-specific rates will later be compared separately in the rural and urban areas.

The overall rate reduction in the first ten-year period was mainly attributed to the older adults (60+). Despite remaining the most vulnerable group in the region, the age-specific suicide rate for those 60–9 and 70+ showed a substantial reduction of 63% and 46%, respectively, for 1983–93. Although the rate then reverted gradually since 1994, the suicide rate for these two age groups in 2003 was lower by 26% and 32%, respectively, when compared with the base year level in 1983.

Elevation in Suicide Rate and Population Aging in Taiwan

Population aging is associated with the rate increase of suicide during 1993 to 2003. From 1983 to 2003, Taiwan underwent a rapid pace of population aging. When the relative size of a higher risk group increases because of population aging, it is inevitable that the overall suicide rate increases. Except for the age group 30–9 that shows a rate increase from 12.1 in the base year 1983 to 17.6 in 2003 (Figure 2), the suicide rate in 2003 for other middle-age groups is close to or is lower than that in 1983. Figure 3 shows the crude suicide rate together with the age standardized suicide rate for the whole period. It indicates that the age-adjusted suicide rate in 2003 was around 13% below the 1983 level. This suggests population aging has been one of the most prominent factors to account for the overall suicide rate increase in Taiwan since 1993.

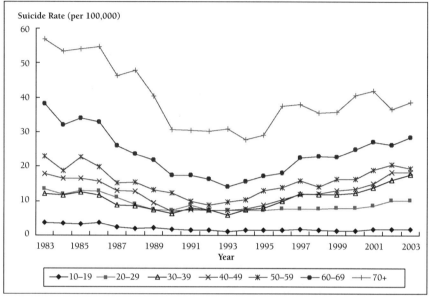

Figure 2   Age-specific suicide rates in Taiwan, 1983–2003.

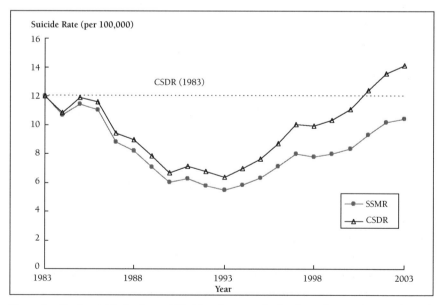

Figure 3   Crude suicide death rate (CSDR) and age-standardized suicide mortality rate (SSMR) in Taiwan, 1983–2003.

Transition in Distribution of Method Used in Taiwan

Figure 4 shows the distribution of suicide method used in Taiwan over the period. It indicates that hanging (E-953) and poisoning (E-950 and E-951) remain the two most commonly used methods. The proportion of poisoning had dropped continuously and substantially from more than 61% in 1983 to around 22% in 2003. In contrast, it shows that hanging became the most common method used for suicide since the early 1990s, and the proportion reached the highest, at 54%, in 1992. Since then, it shows that hanging had also decreased and dropped to approximately 39% by 2003. However, it is worth noting that there has been an increase in suicides through charcoal burning (E-952), which was first introduced from Hong Kong in 1998 (Chan et al. 2005; Yip and Lee 2007) and reached 18% in 2003, and jumping from height (E-957), which increased from 1.5% in 1983 to 11.4% in 2003. These two methods were, respectively, the third and fourth most frequently used suicide methods in Taiwan in 2003.

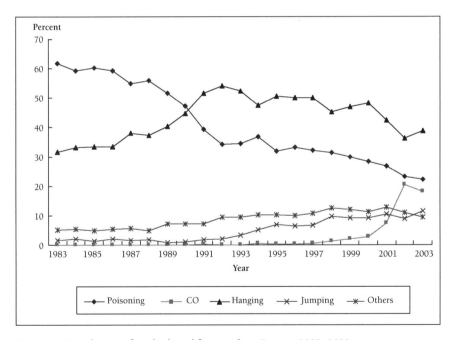

Figure 4   Distribution of method used for suicide in Taiwan, 1983–2003.

Marriage Not a Protection Factor in Taiwan

Figures 5a and 5b present, respectively, male and female suicide rates for four marital groups (unmarried, married, divorced, and widowed), based on data for

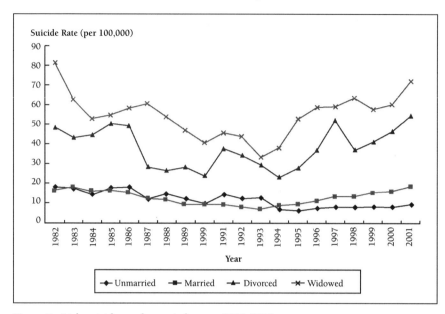

Figure 5a Male suicide rate by marital status, 1982–2001.

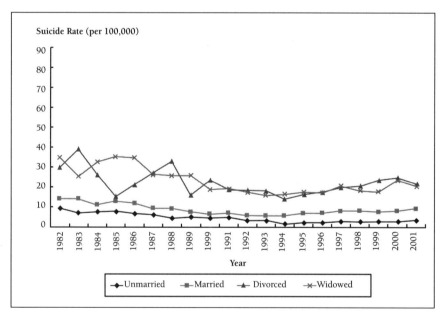

Figure 5b Female suicide rate by marital status, 1982–2001.

the period 1982–2001. For both males and females, widowed and divorced had much higher rates of suicide than the other two groups (married and unmarried). For males, widowed had the highest rate, and the next highest was divorced, whereas for females, widowed and divorced had similar rates after 1991. The unmarried women consistently exhibit low rates (after 1992, the rates are in the range of 1.8 to 3.6 per 100,000) and lower rates than the married (ranging from 5.5 to 9.3 per 100,000 after 1992).

Prior to 1994, the married males had lower rates than the unmarried, but after 1994, the unmarried males became the lowest suicide risk group. Although several studies suggest that marriage could be a protection factor in other societies (Lloyd and Yip 2001; Yip and Thorburn 2004), it appeared that marriage was not a significant protection factor in Taiwan.

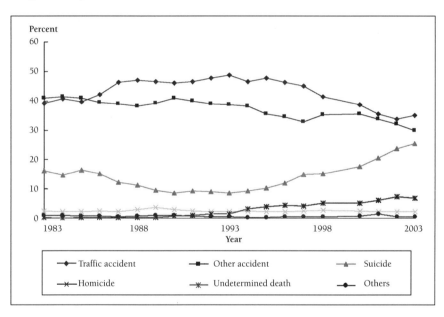

Figure 6 Distribution of external cause for injury and poisoning deaths in Taiwan, 1983–2003.

Suicide: A Leading External Cause of Injury and Poisoning Death in Taiwan

Table 1 gives the ten leading causes of death for the Taiwan in 1983, 1993, and 2003. During this 20-year period, the relative ranking of suicide deaths had increased from the tenth to the ninth leading cause of death. However, when comparing only suicide with injury and poisoning death, we found that suicide had become a major external cause over the period. Figure 6 illustrates the external

Table 1. Ten Leading Causes of Death in Taiwan, 1983, 1993, and 2003.

Rank	1983	1993	2003
1	Diseases of the circulatory system	Diseases of the circulatory system	Neoplasms
2	Neoplasms	Neoplasms	Diseases of the circulatory system
3	Injury and poisoning (excludes suicide)	Injury and poisoning (excludes suicide)	Diseases of the respiratory system
4	Diseases of the digestive system	Symptoms, signs and ill-defined conditions	Endocrine, nutritional and metabolic diseases and immunity disorders
5	Diseases of the respiratory system	Diseases of the digestive system	Diseases of the digestive system
6	Symptoms, signs and ill-defined conditions	Diseases of the respiratory system (excludes suicide)	Injury and poisoning
7	Infectious and parasitic diseases	Endocrine, nutritional and metabolic diseases and immunity disorders	Symptoms, signs and ill-defined conditions
8	Endocrine, nutritional and metabolic diseases and immunity disorders	Infectious and parasitic diseases	Diseases of the genitourinary system
9	Diseases of the genitourinary system	Diseases of the genitourinary system	Suicide
10	Suicide	Suicide	Infectious and parasitic diseases

cause distribution for injury and poisoning death in Taiwan from 1983 to 2003. Although suicide remained the third leading external cause over the whole period, its percentage had gradually increased from the lowest at 8.5% in 1990 to 25.5% in 2003, and tended to converge together with traffic and other accidents during the final stage of the reference period. On the other hand, the increasing proportion of undetermined deaths (from 0.2% in 1983 to 6.9% in 2003) should also be noted in providing information for audiences to evaluate data reliability of the existing reporting system in the Taiwan.

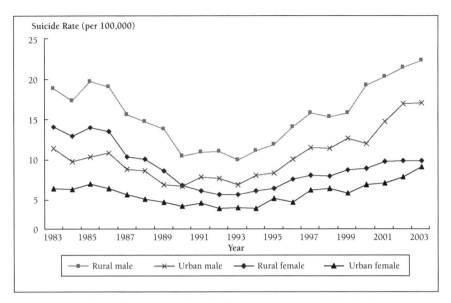

Figure 7 Suicide rates by gender and rural/urban areas of Taiwan, 1983–2003.

Comparisons Between Urban and Rural Taiwan

Under our urban-rural classification modified from Tzeng and Wu (1986), we observed that the regional pattern of suicide death has gradually been shifting from the rural areas to the urban areas over the past two decades, when the percentage in urban Taiwan increased from 45.3% to 60.8%. This has partially been attributed to internal migration and urbanization over the period, increasing the proportion of residents living in urban areas from 60% to 65% during the corresponding period.

Figure 7 shows the gender-specific suicide rates for urban and rural Taiwan from 1983 to 2003. It illustrates that, on average in those 20 years, residents living in rural areas had a higher level of suicidal risk when compared with those living in urban areas. After 1990, a consistent ordering among the four groups is the following (rate from low to high): urban female < rural female < urban male < rural male. When comparing the annual figures across the regions, we see that the relative suicide risk between the urban and rural areas had continuously been reduced from 1.64 in 1983 to 1.30 in 2003 for males, and the change of the corresponding ratio for females was more substantial, from 2.16 to 1.08, over the period.

Figures 8a and 8b give the age-specific suicide rate for males and females in urban and rural Taiwan for the period 1983–2003. They represent further detailed plots of Figure 2. The patterns across the two areas differ mainly in the elderly

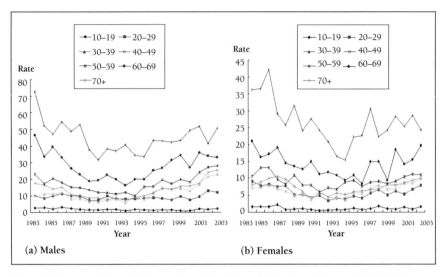

Figure 8a Age-specific suicide rates for male and remale in urban Taiwan, 1983–2003.

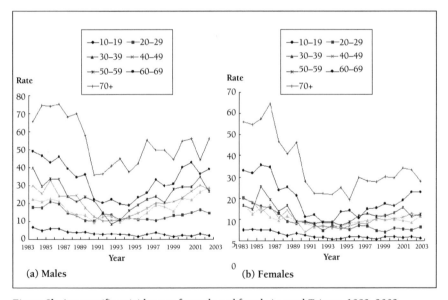

Figure 8b Age-specific suicide rates for male and female in rural Taiwan, 1983–2003.

male groups. The trend for older males aged 70 or above has a significant urban-rural difference for the first ten-year period from 1983 to 1993, in which the suicide rate for this specified group in urban Taiwan showed a moderate but continuous decline, from 72.8 per 100,000 in 1983 to 40.7 in 1993. In contrast, the corresponding figures for rural Taiwan maintained a higher level of around

70 until the late 1980s. Beginning in 1988, the rate showed a rapid and dramatic reduction from 69.9 to a level at 37.6 in 1994. After then, the suicide rates for both areas maintained a relatively stable level for the subsequent years. The rural females generally showed a sharper declining trend than that of the same group in urban areas. This makes a close ratio for urban females and rural females in 2003.

As previously stated, we found that only the 30–9 age group exhibited a significant increase when compared with the rate in the base year of 1983. The urban males had a more pronounced rise than that of the same age group for rural males. Moderate increases were noted for the 40–59 urban males. However, if the year 1993 is used as a baseline, then an upward tendency is evident for all middle-age groups, especially for males.

Figures 9a and 9b give the distribution of suicide methods used in urban and rural Taiwan over the period. The distribution of method used is completely different between the urban and rural areas during these 20 years. In urban Taiwan, the percentage of poisoning was substantially reduced, from about 50% in 1983 to 14.2% in 2003, while hanging has replaced poisoning and become the most commonly used method in urban areas since 1990. Also, it is worth highlighting that charcoal burning has rapidly become a commonly used method. Vividly portrayed by the media as a painless and nonviolent way to end life, the new method has led to a drastic increase in suicides that rapidly generated a new cohort of those committing suicide in urban Taiwan. In 2002, the rate of charcoal burning recorded a dramatic annual increase from 9.1% to 24.6%, making the relative ranking of this method jump to the second highest of the period.

In contrast, the corresponding figures in rural areas have been completely different for the period. The rate of poisoning had also followed a substantial downward trend during the first ten-year period, from more than 70% to 44% in 1993, and hanging became the most commonly used method for suicide. Over the same period, the proportion increased from 24.3% to almost 47%. However, when the share for both methods converged at around 40% in the early 1990s, the transition trend on the pattern of method used tended to maintain at a relatively stable level until 1999. Since 2000, charcoal burning has also gradually become one of the commonly used methods in rural Taiwan.

Figures 10a and 10b show the distribution of external cause for injury and poisoning death for urban and rural Taiwan, respectively. In urban areas, the share of suicide increased from 15% in 1983 to 30.3% in 2003, making this become the most prominent external cause for all injury and poisoning deaths in 2003, when compared with traffic accident (29.5%) and other accidents (28.3%). In addition, the share of undetermined death also increased rapidly from 0.2% to 9% during the same period. On the other hand, in rural Taiwan, the distribution and relative ranking for suicide and other major external causes has maintained at a stable level during that 20 year period.

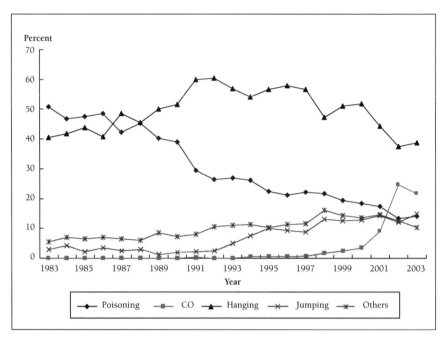

Figure 9a Distribution of suicide methods used in urban Taiwan, 1983–2003.

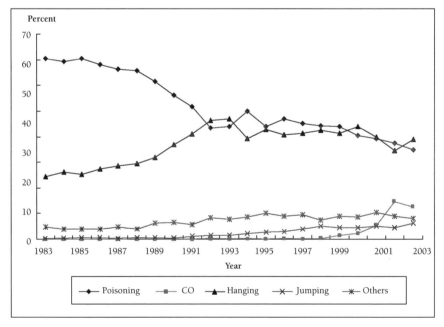

Figure 9b Distribution of suicide methods used in rural Taiwan, 1983–2003.

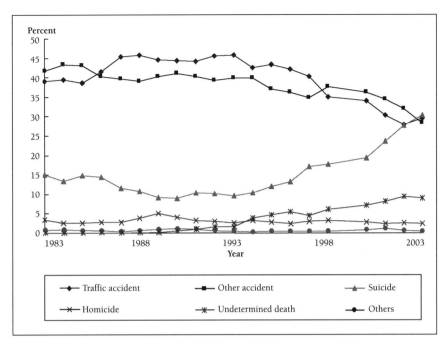

Figure 10a Distribution of external cause for injury and poisoning death in urban Taiwan, 1983–2003.

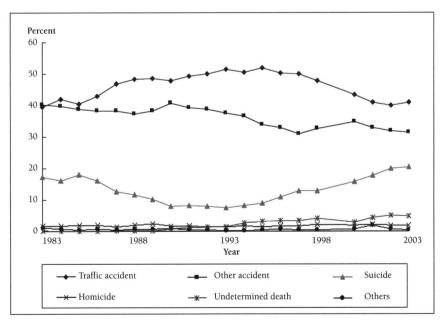

Figure 10b Distribution of external cause for injury and poisoning death in rural Taiwan, 1983–2003.

Discussion

Population Aging Effect

Despite the overall crude suicide rate in Taiwan showing a substantial increase from the early 1990s, the age-standardized suicide rate in Taiwan (Figure 3) has demonstrated that the rise was partly due to the population aging effect over the period. The trend of late marriage, late pregnancy and few children led to a substantial decline in the total fertility rate, from around the replacement level at 2.17 in 1983 to 1.24 in 2003. Taiwan's population underwent fast changes to become an aging society. Concurrently, the child dependency ratio has been reduced by more than 40%, from 0.48 to 0.27, while the corresponding elderly dependency ratio increased from 0.07 to 0.14. (Department of Household Registration Affairs 2006) If the existing age and gender pattern on the suicide rate prevails, (Yip 1996; Yip et al. 2003), the rising trend on the overall rate would prevail in the near future.

Economic Stress: An Essential Role

In exception to the aging effect, it is certain that the age-adjusted suicide rate in Taiwan has followed an upward trend since the mid-1990s. We believe the psychological stress arising from the economic transition has played an essential factor for the suicide rate increase in Taiwan. With the advent of a knowledge-based economy over decades, many unskilled- and labor-intensive positions have been fully replaced with new technologies, making the condition of a less-educated group more difficult in the labor market. More importantly, in order to achieve lower production costs, many Taiwanese manufacturers, in recent decades, have moved their assembly lines into China. This has implicitly accelerated the economic transition and pushed those having a lower socioeconomic status into a more disadvantaged position. Figure 11 illustrates that the crude suicide rate has been closely associated with the unemployment rate over the past 20 years.

A Psychological Autopsy Study

Cheng (1995) and Cheng et al. (2000) conducted a case-controlled psychological autopsy among 113 suicides and 226 living controls matched for age, gender, ethnicity, and area of residence. They used the logistic regression method and found the following significant risk factors:

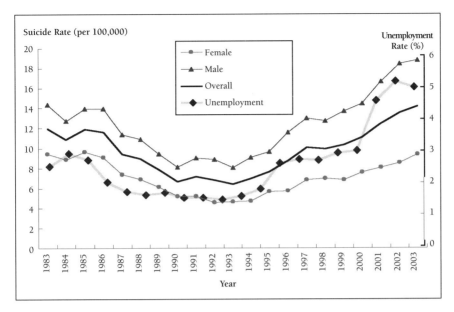

Figure 11 Suicide rates and unemployment rates (%) in Taiwan, 1983–2003.

(1) Loss of events before suicide: suicides experienced the loss of cherished idea, health, close relatives, and material possession.
(2) Family tendency of suicidal behavior: suicides had first-degree relatives with a suicidal behavior (attempted or actual suicide).
(3) Three mental disorders include major depressive episode, emotionally unstable personality disorder, and substance- (e.g., alcohol or drug) dependent disorder.

Role of Mass Media and Internet in Taiwan

In Taiwan, local researchers in the humanities, psychiatry, and journalism have pointed out that the extensive and detailed coverage of suicide-related news on mass media is another major factor relating to suicide in Taiwan (Cheng et al. 2007a). Since 1994, there have been six cable TV news channels in Taiwan. However, these also provide a platform for publicizing suicide and related information to the Taiwanese community, and this contagious effect aggravates the problem. One typical example happened in May 2005 when a male television celebrity committed suicide by hanging; subsequently, the TV channel reiterated that news, continuing for almost two weeks. After the extensive reporting, there was an increase in suicides and also in suicide attempts in the following several weeks (Cheng et al. 2007b). This provides evidence that restrained reporting of suicides is needed for suicide prevention.

The Internet has become a necessity for everyone, yet, this has facilitated a more convenient way to access suicide coverage. In Taiwan, the first suicide completer for charcoal burning learned about that method from the Internet. Thus, it is necessary for the media themselves to set out a guideline for reporting on suicides and related information. Also, the media should take a more active role in raising public awareness for mental health and suicide prevention in Taiwan.

Filicide-Suicides: A Sharp Increase

Filicides are not only family/social tragedies but also serious deprivation of children's rights to live. From 1992 to 2005, there were 198 reported cases of parent-child filicide-suicides in Taiwan (TSPC 2007). About 38% (75 cases) of these cases were carried out by fathers, 51% (101 cases) by mothers and 11% (22 cases) by both. Among the 68 cases of maternal filicide-suicides in 2002_2005, more than half of the cases (35 cases) were committed by charcoal burning. From 1992 to 2000, the average number of reported cases per month is 0.56 (a total of 60 cases in a 9-year period). However, from 2001 to 2005, there were 138 cases, implying the average number of reported cases per month was sharply increased to 2.3 cases per month in this period. A recent investigation of cases in the period of 2005 to 2007 revealed that the average number is further increased to 2.6, and victims are not just infants or small children, but often teenagers (Taiwan Headlines 2007). Besides, media sensationalistic and extensive reports of filicide-suicide cases have caused serious contagious effect. Research on understanding high-risk factors and on setting up more prevention strategies of filicides have become importantly urgent issues in Taiwan.

Control on Pesticides and Fertilizers

Over the past 20 years, we observed a significant reduction in solid and liquid poisoning suicide in Taiwan. This has been accredited to the Council of Agriculture by setting out the Environmental Agents Control Act and related legal ordinance to limit the application and accessibility for about 70 types of pesticides and toxic fertilizers since the 1990s (TACTRI 2007).

Religious Help/Collaboration

In order to promote public awareness of mental health and a positive set of values on life for preventing suicide in Taiwan, local religious groups have put considerable effort in various ways over the past decades. Among those, the Dharma Drum Mountain (DDM) has been one of the most representative organizations in Taiwan. Founded in 1989 by Ven. Sheng Yen, who is one of the most influential Buddhist leaders in Taiwan, the DDM places emphasis on uplifting the character of humanity to build a pure land on earth through the authentic teachings of Buddhism. According to Ven. Sheng Yen, suicide and inflicted self-harm is not allowable under Buddhism. Also, he emphasizes "With Breath There Is Wealth, With Life There Is Hope," and this has deeply impressed people to understand the importance of preventing suicide and eliminating social stigmatization towards depression and other psychiatric disorders. Recently, the DDM foundation launched a website (http://www.no-suicide-no.com) to publicize the message of suicide prevention to the mass audience through the Internet.

Suicide Prevention-Establishment of Taiwan Suicide Prevention Center

In response to the upward trend in suicide rates, the Taiwan Department of Health and Taiwan Association Against Depression established the Taiwan Suicide Prevention Center (TSPC) on December 9, 2005. The mission of TSPC aims to prevent suicide, improve mental health service quality, and organize community support networks nationwide (TSPC 2007). It also provides easily accessible on-line materials and courses for the community to learn about and assist in suicide prevention efforts to promote the messages of "Cherishing Life, Restoring Hope" and "Suicide Prevention is Everybody's Business" (TSPC 2007). Beginning in March 2006, the TSPC publishes a quarterly Newsletter for Suicide Prevention Network. Currently, the TSPC is still under the initial phrase and much could be learned from the experiences of Hong Kong and neighboring districts in the region.

7

Thailand

Manote Lotrakul

Thailand has a relatively low suicide rate compared with several other Asian countries, with a rate of 6.8 per 100,000. However, the rate has also increased significantly in the past five years. The age group of 25–44 years had the highest rate. There is a significant geographical difference in suicide rates. The relatively deprived regions — north and central Thailand — have a higher suicide rate than that of the south. Apparently, religion has been a protective factor of suicide in Thailand. Some suicide prevention programs in Thailand are discussed.

Introduction

Thailand has a relatively low suicide rate compared with several other Asian countries. However, since the Asian economic crisis in 1997, the suicide rate has dramatically increased, and suicide has become a major public health issue for the country. Very few reports on suicide in Thailand have been published internationally. The last data on suicide trends in Thailand documented in a World Health Organization (WHO) report was in 1994 (1999). Furthermore, the suicide pattern in Thailand is somewhat different from that of other Asian countries. This chapter examines recent national trends and patterns of suicide in Thailand.

Geographically, Thailand is the heart of Southeast Asia. Roughly the size of France, Thailand is composed of four main regions: the north, the northeast, the central plain, and the south. At midyear 2007, Thailand has an estimated population of 62.8 million people (male 31.0 million, female 31.8 million), with 64% living in rural areas. The crude birth rate is 12.7 per 1,000 population, and the crude death rate is 8.0 per 1,000 population. Life expectancy at birth has increased over the past two decades to reach 68.4 years for males and 75.2 years for females (Institute for Population and Social Research 2007).

Theravada Buddhism is the national religion that is practiced by 95% of the population. The rest of the population practices Islam, Christianity, Hinduism, or other faiths. The official national language, spoken by almost 100% of the population, is Thai. Significant influential ethnic groups are the Chinese and Thai-Chinese, both who are disproportionately concentrated in the urban areas. About 4% of the population aged 60 and over *identify* themselves as Chinese and another 9% as Thai-Chinese (Chayovan and Knodel 1997). The majority of Thai people are matrilocal. Parents prefer to live with a married daughter rather than a married son, notably in the northern and northeastern regions. Children typically inherit equally, except for the one who stays with the parents, and who commonly gains the house. In contrast, Thai-Chinese tend to be patrilineal and patrilocal. (Sobieszczyk, Knodel, and Napaporn 2003).

Agriculture is the traditional backbone of the economy. Thailand is one of the world's biggest producers of rice. Thailand's industrial sector includes electrical appliances, furniture, integrated circuits, and plastics. Tourism has been the country's leading source of foreign exchange since the early 1980s and has been a major contributor to growth in the service sector.

Mortality Ascertainment in Thailand

In Thailand, a death is registered at the place of occurrence. According to the 1991 Civil Registration Act, a person who discovers a death is required to notify the local registrar within 24 hours (or seven days in remote areas); failure to do so results in a fine of up to 1,000 baht (US$30), which is equivalent to six times the daily minimum wage. Reporting of deaths gradually improved after the implementation of the act (Tangcharoensathien et al. 2006).

When a death occurs in a hospital, a medical death certificate is issued by health personnel. For a death that occurs outside of the hospital, a death notification report will be issued by a local registrar (village head or health center personnel). Both the medical health certificate and the death notification report are to be sent to the district registrar to issue the death certificate. This death certificate will be the basis for registration at a District or Municipality Office. Thai legislation also requires that the cause of death be reported in every instance. Suicide is regarded as an unnatural death that, as required by law, is subject to forensic investigation and is to be approved by police officers and physicians.

The Ministry of Interior is responsible for registering deaths at the local administrative level. Data registries from death certificates are then compiled electronically and submitted to the Bureau of Registration Administration, Ministry of Interior. The Ministry of Public Health has full access to this national database and is responsible for processing the vital statistics data for the whole country and for disseminating, on an annual basis, the information in the Report of Public Health Statistics.

There are two gaps that contribute to incomplete death registration: the gap between the death event and its certification, and the gap between death certification and its registration. The deceased may be brought to burial with neither a death certificate nor a death registration (especially in very remote areas), or the certificate may be available, but the death has not been registered. A death certificate alone being sufficient, a death registration is not required for facilitating religious and funeral arrangements. This contributes to a lack of completion of death registration in the national statistical data (Tangcharoensathien et al. 2006).

Recently, there was a study to verify causes of death in death registries. The authors used the verbal autopsy method, together with an analysis of medical records and reviews by panels of physicians, to assess internal consistency. The study was conducted in 15 sample provinces during 1997–99. Results showed that data from the vital registration system identified suicide as a cause of death for 1.3% of total deaths, whereas the verbal autopsy method found that suicide contributes up to 1.9% of total causes of death (Choprapawan 2003). This difference may be explained partly by the fact that doctors or health personnel may not record a death as a suicide to spare the victim and his/her family the social stigma sometimes associated with a death by suicide.

In this report, data from the Bureau of Policy and Strategy, Ministry of Public Health, were used to analyze mortality from suicide with an emphasis on the last five years of available data. Detailed information included rate, age, gender, and suicide methods.

Suicide statistics in 1994 were considered unreliable and were excluded from this analysis because the rate was unusually low and the patterns of suicide were notably different from other years. For example, suicides by hanging were less than 5% — a rate that is much lower than any other year. This deviation was due to the change in the cause-of-death coding system in Thailand from the International Classification of Diseases, Ninth Revision (ICD-9) to the tenth edition (ICD-10). The suicide rate decrease in 1997 was due to a change in the method of data entering, from one that was handled by post mail to one that is electronically transferred.

Suicide Trends

The suicide rates in Thailand for the period 1977—2005 are given in Figure 1.

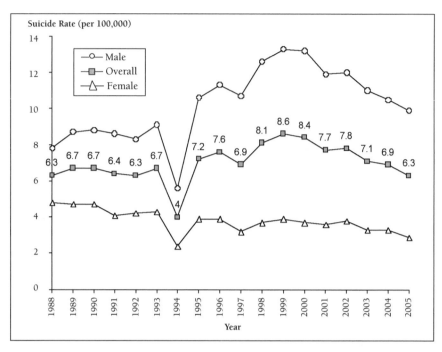

Figure 1   Suicide rates by gender, 1977–2005, Thailand.

From 1993 onwards, total suicide rates increased up to a peak of 8.6 per 100,000 (5,290 suicides) in 1999, after which they decreased to 6.3 per 100,000 in 2005 (Figure 1). The average suicide rate between 2001 and 2005 was 7.2 per 100,000, whereas between 1996 and 2000, the average suicide rate was only 7.92 per 100,000.

The increase in suicide rates during 1995-2000 is suggested to be related to the economic crisis of 1997. There was a sharp slash in the annual economic growth from 7 to -1.7 in 1997 and -10.8 in 1998. During 1998, the Thai economy contracted by 10.2%. The crisis resulted in substantial losses in social welfare. The effect of this financial downfall, extended throughout Asia and became a starting point of the so-called "Asian economic crisis." More than one million Thais fell below the poverty line as a result of the crisis. The unemployment rate increased from 2% of the total labor force in 1996 to 5% in 1998, and 5.3% in 1999 (World Bank 2001; Wibulpolprasert et al. 2002). Suicide rates in 1999 were at their highest peak (5,290) in all of Thailand's history.

The economic crisis resulted in a higher unemployment rate, leading to an increase in suicidal ideas. Telephone surveys conducted between 1997 and 2000 by the Department of Mental Health revealed that the prevalence of stress and suicidal ideas among the unemployed were approximately two-fold higher than that in the employed and general public (Department of Mental Health 2000).

Chartananondh et al. (1999) studied the stress felt by Thai people during this period and found that people in north and central Thailand were most affected by the economic downturn.

Thailand entered a recovery stage in the last quarter of 1999. Real GDP of the country grew by 4.2% in 1999 and 4.4% in 2000, largely due to strong exports that increased about 20% in 2000. The higher unemployment rates in 1998 and 1999 caused by the crisis fell slightly as a consequence of economic recovery. The economic recovery, witnessed by the gains in real wages, reduced the likelihood of deep and lasting reduction in living standards (World Bank 2001). The suicide rate started to decline from 8.6 per 100,000 in 1999 to 6.3 per 100,000 in 2005.

Age

Table 1 shows suicide rates by age group for the period between 1996 and 2005. The highest suicide rates were found in the early adult period. Suicides were highest in the age group 25–29.

Table 1. Suicide Rates (per 100,000) by Age Group, 1996–2005, Thailand

	15–9	20–4	25–9	30–4	35–9	40–4	45–9	50–4	55–9	60–4	65–9	70–4	75+
1996	9.5	13.6	12.8	13.3	10.3	8.1	8.0	7.0	6.5	8.3	8.4	7.9	6.4
1997	8.1	11.7	12.2	11.5	10.0	8.5	8.2	6.9	6.6	6.3	7.5	5.9	6.7
1998	8.9	13.6	14.7	13.5	11.7	9.4	8.8	8.1	8.8	8.6	7.8	8.4	6.5
1999	8.4	13.7	16.0	13.6	11.8	11.0	9.1	9.1	8.9	9.9	9.5	9.8	9.7
2000	7.5	13.7	15.1	13.5	12.4	11.9	9.1	9.1	8.4	10.2	7.4	8.1	10.8
2001	5.6	12.1	13.4	12.5	11.5	10.8	9.2	8.2	7.1	10.1	7.9	10.9	10.5
2002	6.4	11.2	12.5	10.8	10.0	9.8	9.3	9.7	8.9	10.1	10.0	10.8	9.6
2003	5.0	9.4	9.6	10.5	9.8	9.4	8.5	8.9	9.5	9.5	10.8	8.8	8.7
2004	4.7	8.1	10.0	10.4	10.0	9.0	8.1	9.2	9.2	8.1	9.2	11.3	9.0
2005	4.1	7.6	9.4	9.3	8.9	8.1	8.3	6.9	9.4	8.5	7.3	10.3	8.1

Figure 2 demonstrates that during the period between 1992 and 2005, suicide rates were consistently highest in the age group 25–44. It is notable that suicide rates in both the 15–24 year age group and the 25–44 year age group started to decrease since the year 2000, whereas the rate in the adult population of age 45 onwards showed an increasing trend.

Suicides in young adults, particularly in adult males, have been most prevalent in Thailand for decades, whereas elderly suicide rates have been modest. This figure is in contrast to the West, where suicide risk rises with advancing age (Bertolote and Fleischman 2002). Findings from other Asian places, such as China,

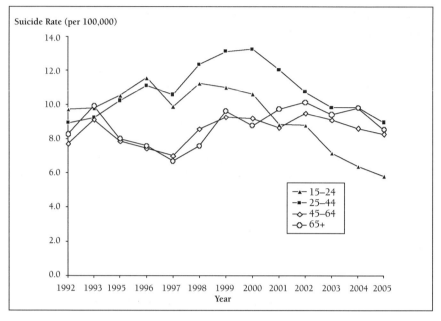

Figure 2   Suicide rates by age, 1992–2005, Thailand.

Hong Kong, Japan, and Singapore, also indicate that suicide rates are positively correlated with age (Pritchard 1996; Takahashi et al. 1998; Yip and Tan 1998).

The fact that elderly people in Thailand are better protected against suicide, compared with those in other countries, may be due to some social values in Thai society. Respect for seniority in age is an integral part of Thai culture, and, traditionally, elderly persons are treated with respect. Children feel a moral obligation to take care of aging parents. Most Thai people are Buddhists who believe in the concept of repayment for their parents' goodness and usually live with their parents (Choowattanapakorn 1999). Elderly adults do not feel bad for having to depend on their children for financial support. Parents, however, also typically feel a continuing obligation to ensure their children's well-being. Exchange of support and services between parents and adult children are prominent in Thailand, as in much of the developing world. Living arrangements of older aged parents and adult children are closely linked to this system of support exchange. A vast majority of older Thais either live with or very near at least one of their adult children (Knodel et al. 2000). Siriboon's (1993) survey of young Thais concerning their role and attitude about care-taking of aging parents found that most people frequently and consistently take care of aging parents; they are willing and are happy to do so until their aging parents die. Statistically, more female than male aging parents tend to receive more care and support from their children.

Recently, there was a survey using a stratified two-stage sampling procedure to examine the level of happiness and subjective well-being among 986 subjects aged 55–88 years in the central part of Thailand. Results revealed that 32.3% of them lived with their children and relatives, and 44.7% lived with their spouses and relatives. Most of them were satisfied with their family and neighborhood. Most of them had positive attitudes towards the future, as the mean score of future happiness was higher than current happiness, and 80% of them were confident in their perception (Gray et al. 2006).

Regarding the prevalence of suicides in young adults in Thailand, one should note that the suicide peak during early adulthood is an issue of serious concern, as that age group is the major productive force of the country. In comparison to Western countries that have suicide rates similar to Thailand's, the health impact of suicide in Thailand, as measured by the potential years of life lost (PYLL) and which takes into account the number of potential years left to live at each age of death, is undoubtedly greater.

A report of findings from a national burden of diseases and injury study in Thailand during 1999 (Thai working group on burden of disease and injuries 2002) showed that suicide is the ninth leading cause of the disability-adjusted life year (DALY) in men. Among the leading causes of years of life lost due to premature death (YLL), suicide ranked 7th in men and 14th in women. The relative YLL burden for suicide in males doubles that of females (4% versus 2%).

Gender

In Thailand, the suicide rate in men is higher than that in women. The male-female suicide ratio increased steadily from 1.6:1 in 1988 to the highest ratio of 3.6:1 in 2000. The average male-female suicide ratio for the period between 2001– and 2005 was 3.3:1.

Figure 3 shows that the suicide rates that rose substantially during the period of economic crisis were largely accounted for by an increase in male suicides. Among females, suicide rates decreased over time.

Figure 4 shows the average suicide rates categorized by age and gender during 1996–2000 and during 2001–05. Suicide trends were the same for both periods. Male suicide rates were higher than female rates for all ages. The highest rate of male suicides occurred in those aged 25–9 years, followed by a small peak after age 70 years. Among females, suicide rates showed less variation with age.

Suicide rates in males have continually increased between 1996 and 2000, particularly suicide rates in early adult males during the economic crisis, while female suicides were less affected by the crisis. This incident results in the widening gap between genders.

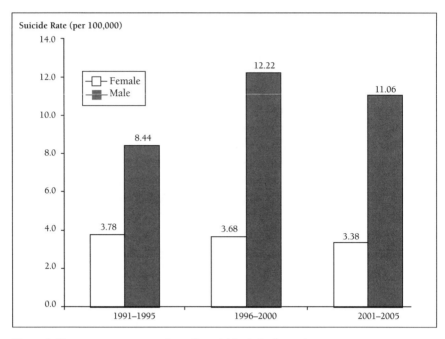

Figure 3 Five-year average annual rate for suicides in both genders.

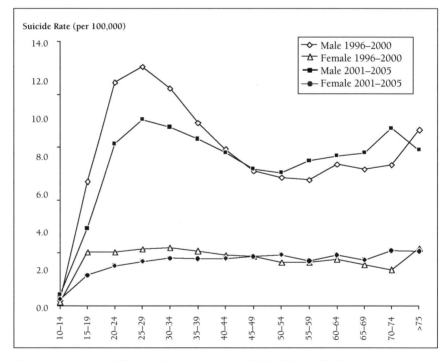

Figure 4 Average suicide rates by age and gender, 1996–2000, 2001–05.

These data implied that males may cope less well than females with the stress of social change, especially in early adulthood, a time when people begin to get married and start to have more responsibilities. A recent qualitative study of subjects with severe suicide attempts in the north of Thailand found that important factors associated with suicide attempts among males included frequent quarrels with parents, chaotic sexual relationship, poor coping skills, and the use of alcohol to reduce stress. Among females, common stressors arose from unhappy love affairs and domestic violence. In other words, problems in males reflected "inner" problems, i.e., maladaptive lifestyles, whereas problems in females indicated "outer" problems, i.e., gender inequality (Lotrakul 2005). It would be interesting to study further whether these findings would also apply to the completed suicide population.

Methods of Suicide

Hanging has been the most common means of suicide for both genders over the decade (Table 2). Of all suicides, suicide by hanging increased substantially from 43.5% between 1992 and 1997 to 58.3% between 2001 and 2005; however, suicide by self-poisoning decreased from 29% between 1992 and1997 to 25.6% between 2001 and 2005. Suicide by hanging increased both in proportion to all suicides and in absolute number of cases. From 1997, suicide by hanging in females, which previously had been low, began to rise above self-poisoning and continued to be the most frequent method of suicide employed by females. Suicide by hanging was also the most common method across all age ranges. For suicide by self-poisoning, agricultural chemicals were the most frequently used substances. Suicide by firearms did not change much over the decade.

Table 2. Percentages of Methods of Suicide by Gender: 1996–2000 and 2001–05.

	1996–2000		2001–05	
	Males	Females	Males	Females
Hanging	55.6	47.6	60.9	50.0
Agriculture chemicals	7.4	11.9	14.8	24.5
Toxic substances	10.9	19.5	2.8	4.8
Drugs	2.7	4.9	4.4	7.9
Firearms	5.9	1.7	4.8	0.9
Others	17.5	14.3	12.3	11.8

As in most Asian countries, hanging is the most prevalent method of suicide in Thailand. Hanging is a highly lethal method of suicide. Reports from developed countries estimated that the fatality rate of this method is over 70% (Aufderheide et al. 1994). The mortality rate may even be higher in Thailand because of a long distance between hospitals, a dearth of doctors in rural areas and less well-equipped rural hospitals.

One effective strategy in reducing suicide rates is to restrict access to the means of suicide (Lindesay 1986; Marzuk et al. 1992). However, a systematic review by Gunnell et al. (2005) concluded that this measure is of limited value. They recommend that strategies should focus on the prevention of suicide in controlled environments, such as prisons and psychiatric hospitals, on the emergency management of "near-hanging" and on the primary prevention of suicide in general.

Intake of agricultural chemicals is the second most frequently employed method of suicide. In Thailand, pesticides (including insecticides, herbicides, and fungicides) are easily available in rural areas, particularly during harvesting and planting. Almost all pesticides used in Thailand are imported, and these imports have increased rapidly over the past decade. A project implemented by Thailand's Office of the National Environment Board (2000) reported that pesticide poisoning was due primarily to occupational exposure (46%), suicide (36%), accidental poisoning (6%), and residues on food (2%) (Thapinta and Hudak 1998). The occupational figure reflects a heavy usage of pesticides, with inadequate safety precautions. The widely used agricultural substance for suicide is methomyl, which is a broad-spectrum carbamate insecticide. Besides having a faint odor, methomyl is water-soluble and is easily available. These factors make it the most commonly used agricultural chemical for suicide (Narongchai 1995).

The study by Mongkol (2003), in seven provinces of Thailand, found that most suicidal behavior, both completed and attempted suicide, were impulsive acts. Nearly 80% of the subjects had no suicidal plan. The methods used by subjects were those that were readily available at the time of acute distress. In rural Thailand, it is easier to find a pesticide than to find medicines, such as paracetamol, as most farmers keep their own supply of pesticides in or close to their homes. A study in Sri Lanka by Eddleston et al. (2006) found that those who attempted suicide used pesticide because of its easy availability. There was no difference in reasons for choices of poison among people ingesting different poisons, despite marked differences in toxicity.

Finding measures that restrict access to toxic pesticides is an important issue for these subjects. Results from many studies suggested that restricting the availability of toxic pesticides reduced the number of deaths from poisoning (Eddleston et al. 2002). The government should try to limit the availability of agricultural chemicals and educate farmers about the safe purchase, transportation, storage, usage, and disposal of pesticides.

Marital Status

A study of 241 subjects who had succeeded in committing suicide in northern Thailand found that 33.6% were married, while 31.5% were single, 11.2% separated, 7.9% widowed, and 10.4% divorced (Tantipiwatanaskul et al. 1998). Another recent study found that, among suicide subjects studied, 54.4% were married, 34.9% single, 5.8% widowed, and 4.9% separated or divorced (Mongkol et al. 2005).

Studies from Western countries have shown that marriage protects against suicide. Married persons experience the lowest suicide rates. Suicide is common among single individuals, followed by those who are divorced, separated, and widowed. It has been proposed that a lower risk of suicide associated with married status may result from the protective effect of marriage itself. Marriage provides social and emotional stability, whereas divorce, separation, singlehood, and widowhood do not (Qin et al. 2003; Kreitman 1988; Kposowa 2000; Yip 1998).

Findings from Tantipiwatanaskul et al. (1998) and Mongkol et al. (2005) do not support this notion, as most of their suicide subjects were married. This is in line with other studies from Asian countries (Phillips et al. 2002; Vijayakumar et al. 2005). In Thailand, most of those who are single still live with their own extended family so they are neither alone nor lack psychological support. Regarding the issue that marriage provides emotional stability, it can be argued that marriage can also be a source of distress, especially for wives in a society where gender inequity is still prevalent. Studies of rural young women in China reported that the majority of the suicides were related to family conflicts (Zhang et al. 2004; Phillips et al. 1999). For example, a study of 260 completed suicide samples found that 47% of reasons given for committing suicide were confrontation between husband and wife and wife abuse (Zhang et al. 2004). Spouse violence in Thai society is a problem that has been ignored until recently due to the socio-cultural structure and gender bias. Although abused women often live in terror, many are trapped by fear of community disapproval.

In Thailand, society sets a belief that the problem between a wife and husband is like that between teeth and tongue, which are normally in conflict. When a wife has marital problems or faces family violence, she is expected to be submissive. Domestic violence is commonly viewed as a "family affair" and, therefore, private. This belief is reinforced in the teaching *"fai nai ya nam o'k, fai n'ok ya nam khao,"* which literally means "The inside fire should not be taken out, the outside fire should not be brought in." This implies that people should not talk about family problems to others no matter how stressful they are. A recent study of attempted suicide in northern Thailand showed that unhappy love affairs and domestic violence were two main problems in female samples (Lotrakul et al. 2000). The author concurs with Vijayakumar (2008) that this issue needs to be addressed and further explored, as marriage and family dynamics in Asian societies are much different from those of the West.

Geographical Distribution

During the 2001–05 period, suicide rates were highest in the northern region (12.0 per 100,000), followed by the central (8.0 per 100,000), the south (5.7 per 100,000), and the northeast (5.0 per 100,000). From 1997 onwards, suicide rates increased in all regions, but the rise in the north was prominent (Figures 5 and 6). Most of the provinces with high suicide rates were in the upper northern Thailand. After 1999, suicide rates in most regions, except the south, began to decline.

Provinces with high suicide rates were provinces in the upper north whose people are generally perceived to be peace-loving, gentle, kind, and hospitable. Chiang Mai, the principal northern city, is one of the most attractive cities for tourists as well as Thai people. However, it has the second highest average suicide rates (2001–05) after its southern sister city, Lamphun. This figure suggests that such perceptions may be incorrect. The outcome measures of quality of life, such as HIV infection, alcohol consumption, and suicide, are worse in the north (Fordham 1995; Isarabhakdi 1995; Lotrakul 2005). These may indicate that life is not satisfying for them.

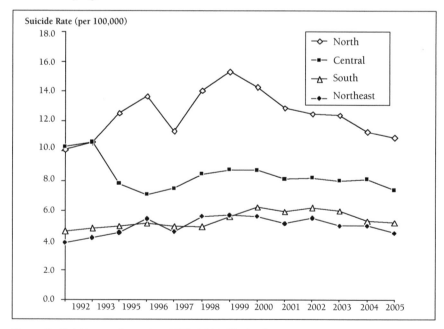

Figure 5   Suicide rates by region, 1992–2005, Thailand.

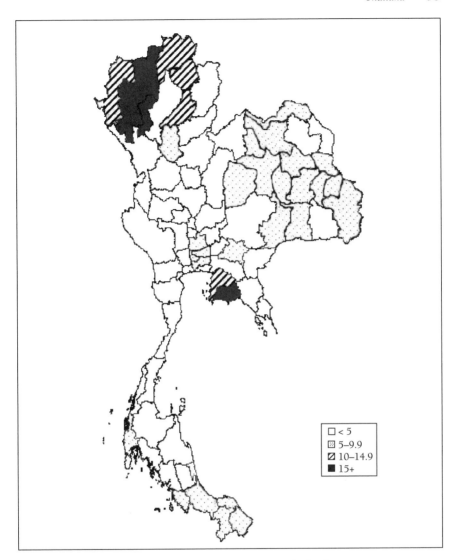

Figure 6 Suicide rates (per 100,000) by provinces, 2005, Thailand.

Other Associated Factors

Precipitating Events

Recently, Mongkol et al. (2005) collected information from 811 patients who died after being admitted with attempted suicide. More than one precipitating event could be identified. Data revealed that interpersonal relationships were the most common sources of immediate stress (54.6%). The reported events were:

feeling hurt at being scolded (23.1%); failed love affair, jealousy (11.2%); family dispute (16.2%); and unmet need for attention (4.1%). A total of 12.3% had psychotic disorders as the primary factor determining suicide, followed by depressive disorder (10.4%), alcohol-related problems (7.5%), and drug dependence (2.5%). Chronic medical illnesses and HIV/AIDS accounted for 13.1%. Only 10% of the events were due to financial problems. Precipitating causes of suicide were multiple, rather than a single factor.

These findings were comparable to those reported from China (Zhang et al. 2004; Phillips et al. 2002). Psychiatric disorders in this study were not as common as those found in Western countries. This may be partly due to differences in study methods.

Religious Beliefs

In non-Buddhist religious practices, individuals' faith in God may serve as a protective factor against suicide because it creates cognitive dissonance in those who believe a higher God creates life, and individuals do not have the right to extinguish that life, even if it is their own (Neeleman et al. 1998). However, Thai Buddhists avoid committing suicide because they are afraid of the consequences of this sinful act. In Thai Buddhist thought, two principles are involved in the suicidal act: karma and rebirth.

Thai people believe in karma — that the past produces a major impact on the present. There are inescapable results of our actions. They believe that rebirth occurs not only within this human realm. There are also heavenly realms and lower realms: realms of animals and realms of spirits and demons. We may experience a number of incarnations in various realms. The present life is simply a part of the unending cycle of birth and consequent decay and death (*samsara*), which stretches out across space and time.

Karma may be experienced here and now or may be experienced upon rebirth — karma ripening in the next life. There are two aspects of karma: good karma, which leads to positive/pleasurable experiences, such as high rebirth (as a deva, or human); and bad karma, which results in suffering and low rebirth (as a hell-sufferer or as an animal). One may be reborn as other types of beings according to the karmic quality of each individual and, particularly, according to the person's emotional state at the last stage of consciousness of his life. Even if the character of the new life is affected by the whole previous life, the nature of the last conscious state still contributes significantly to the quality of the ensuing one. If it is wholesome (*kusala*), this will produce a wholesome inauguration of the new life. Similarly, if it is unwholesome (*akusala*), the ensuing new life will be unwholesomely inaugurated (Ratanakul 2004).

Buddhism's first precept states that one should refrain from taking the life of living beings. Within this precept, killing one's life is the gravest offence a Buddhist can commit. According to *samsara,* one cannot avoid suffering by taking his life, nor can a person escape from the "wheel of suffering" by doing so. Moreover, the emotional states at the dying moment of those who commit suicide are mostly negative ones, e.g., anger, fear, bitter, hatred, and jealousy. Ultimately, both of these will lead them to the planes of loss and woe or the lower world (*Apàyabhåmi*) and, hence, further suffering.

These beliefs prevail among Thai people and buffer them from the risks associated with suicidal behavior. However, beliefs may not be a concern for those who committed suicide impulsively because the action usually is performed with little or no time to reconsider.

Cultural Factors

In some cultures, suicide is permissible in certain situations and can be perceived as normal. For example, in Japan, suicide is sometimes considered an honorable action. It is often seen as a kind of atonement or a way of taking responsibility. Scandal-tainted politicians and businessmen often make headlines by killing themselves. Takahashi et al. (1998) explained that Japanese place a high value on group cohesiveness. They cannot tolerate the feeling of being excluded from a group of significant others. Committing suicide is a form of taking responsibility for causing trouble to the organization.

Although Thai people are somewhat socialized to be interdependent, connected and concerned with others, and constantly aware of the relationships as the Japanese are (Kitayama and Markus 1994), Thai people do not give such high priority to group unity. The act of committing suicide to show responsibility seldom happens in Thailand. What happens more often is suicide to escape from debt, from financial problems, or from being found guilty.

"Go die" and "Noi Jai"

Results from a qualitative study done in the north of Thailand illustrates that the subject of suicide is a term that is a part of daily life (Lotrakul et al. 2000). The expression "Go die" is used as an idiom to communicate the distress being experienced. Not infrequently, when there is a quarrel between family members, the one who is more senior or superior will tell the other to "Go die." Tragically, sometimes that person does commit suicide impulsively, out of disappointment or anger, using an available indoor toxic substance.

A term that is frequently heard from those with suicidal behavior is *Noi Jai*, which is used to express the emotion state of feeling hurt, disappointed, and angry because a person is ignored, rejected or does not get as much attention as expected. It is used in a situation when a person expects that another person will indulge him or her and, as socially accepted, it is the obligation of the second person to do so, whether or not he or she wants to. Following are examples of common scenarios of suicide cases coming to an emergency room. An adolescent feels *Noi Jai* and takes pesticides after being scolded by her parents for coming home late, going out at night, or having a boyfriend. A woman, whose husband goes out with his friends every night, feels *Noi Jai* and ingests household cleaners after her husband has gone out again, even though she is sick. *Noi Jai* is not limited only to a woman or a subordinate. Parents can *Noi Jai* their children for neglecting them and a husband can *Noi Jai* his wife for her always going back to visit her parents, despite being married for some time.

HIV/AIDS

Provinces with high suicide rates are those in the upper north. One important factor associated with suicide is HIV infection, which is also most prevalent in the north. A study by Somboontanont et al. (2000) in Chiangmai province during 1996–98 revealed that the two most important factors related to suicide were HIV infection and financial problems. Tantipiwatanaskul and Visrutratana (1998) conducted a psychological autopsy study in Chiangmai, a province with the highest suicide rate, and found that the five most common precipitating factors were HIV infection (20%), alcohol-related problems (18.7%), marital discord (17.8%), chronic illnesses (17.8%), and financial problems (15.8). The HIV infection rate in each area in this region correlated significantly with the suicide rate. HIV/AIDS related problems were in 39% of the cases investigated. Compared with those without HIV/AIDS related problems, HIV/AIDS subjects were more likely to be younger ($p < .001$), had previously attempted suicide ($p < .05$), had more depression ($p < .01$), and had fewer alcohol problems ($p < .01$).

A study by the Asia Pacific Network of People Living with HIV/AIDS (APN+) found that a quarter of the people living with HIV/AIDS in Thailand reported being insulted and harassed because of their HIV status (United Nations Development Program 2004). Some people with HIV still have to contend with their HIV status being disclosed to family members or neighbors without their consent.

Thailand's AIDS epidemic is severe; success in overcoming it requires joint efforts among government, private sector, and civil society. Each partner in this effort brings a comparative advantage in addressing different aspects of the problem. At present, Thailand is widely regarded as a showcase in the struggle against HIV/AIDS.

Since the study by Tantipiwatanaskul and Visrutratana (1998), there has been no other psychological autopsy study of suicide in provinces in the upper north. Anecdotal evidence from local health care personnel suggests that the current HIV/AIDS problem is not as severe as a decade ago. In Thailand, access to HIV/AIDS medical care has been made available since the early 1990s and has shifted to many new therapies over time. According to the new health policy, the number of patients gaining access to treatment has been increasing considerably, from 3,600 cases in 2001 to 50,752 cases in 2004. After the Thai Government Pharmaceutical Organization (GPO) launched generic versions of essential anti-retrovirals in 2001, the cost of treatment has been reduced significantly. At present, the yearly cost of anti-retroviral medications in Thailand is US$300 compared to US$8,000 in the EU countries (Department of Diseases Control 2006).

Suicide Prevention

After the economic crisis of 1997, the Department of Mental Health, Ministry of Public Health, implemented a series of suicide prevention initiatives to reduce the risks of suicide. Examples of these included the establishment of the crisis intervention centers; organizing a seminar on guidelines for the reporting of suicidal behavior in the media; promoting public awareness of depression, suicidal behavior and warning signs; and conducting a depression awareness and training program for general practitioners around the country.

These projects were listed as top priority programs of the Department of Mental Health. Examples of related programs that have been established for some time are: a toll-free 24-hour nationwide 1223 hotline network with cooperation from the Telephone Organization of Thailand; the "To be Number One Friend Corner" — a program to promote interconnectedness and to improve life-skills among youth, both in schools and in the community; AIDS counseling services in community hospitals nationwide; and the suicide surveillance system in the northern region. For the last five years, there has been a one-hour, weekly television talk show hosted by a popular male psychiatrist discussing various mental health issues. The department also supports a three-hour, nightly, call-in, counseling radio program in Bangkok and a weekly, local radio program on mental health issues. It can be said that, during the past five years, Thai people have been made more aware of depression and its association with suicidal behavior.

In 2005, the Thai government announced the "Healthy Thailand" plan, which is an important policy for building a healthy public. Of the 17 policies, one clearly states that the suicide rates are to be reduced.

Recently, the Department of Mental Health has announced the suicide prevention strategic plan for 2005–08, , which includes:.

1. Promote the general public awareness and understanding of depression and suicide.

   Examples of activities are: launching the third annual national suicide prevention day 2006 and the third annual national depression awareness day; conducting a "train the trainers" workshop on suicide prevention and depression awareness for faith community leaders; holding a seminar on "the role of media in preventing suicide."

2. Enhance the effectiveness of helping teams, both clinical and professional practice.

   Examples of activities are: conducting a workshop on suicide prevention for general practitioners; supporting the capacity of building programs for counselors; and organizing a workshop on policy and program development and administration.

3. Improve the record system.

   Examples of activities are: developing protocols for collecting information on suicide deaths and nonfatal attempts and training-related personnel; and creating a homepage (http://www.suicidethai.com) to collect and disseminate materials and statistical data on suicide.

4. Improve knowledge and promote suicide-related research.

   Examples of activities are: holding the sixth annual conference on depression and suicide prevention in 2007; supporting local community initiatives; and supporting and promoting studies on adolescent suicides.

The Department of Mental Health, Ministry of Public Health, is the government organization that is responsible for much of the mental health of the whole nation. In the early years, almost all of the suicide prevention projects were organized and carried out by the department personnel. In 2001, the department expanded its projects to cover half of the country, and in 2006, the projects covered 76 provinces nationwide. The department sought cooperation with health care personnel at the provincial level, community leaders, and local teachers. However, all activities are performed under the supervision of the department, which sometimes is influenced by political interests.

Most of the suicide prevention programs still have the primary focus within the health care system. There are few collaborations between the public and private sectors. Similar to other governmental health promotion efforts in Thailand, it has suffered from the common problems of centralization, bureaucratic compartmentalization, and a rigid budgetary system (Moodie et al. 2000).

Currently, nongovernmental organizations (NGOs) are involved in a number of health programs, and the majority of them engage in HIV/AIDS problems, child health, and health service systems. Generally, to date there has been no active and influential NGO devoted to mental health issues in Thailand.

As with other developing countries, there are common problems of staff shortage and budget constraints. Local health care personnel are burdened with various assigned projects from the central bureaus. This problem limits their capacity to initiate additional prevention projects and sometimes affects the quality of the program.

Regarding the above limitations, instead of investing resources in multiple, universal prevention programs, the projects should be redirected to focus on high-risk individuals and use the interventions that have best evidence support of effectiveness, e.g., education of physician and gatekeeper, and restriction of access to lethal means of suicide (Mann et al. 2005; Beautrais 2006).

Conclusions

The overall suicide rates in Thailand are not as high as in many other Asian countries, but suicide has a larger effect than what is generally perceived because the highest proportion of suicide cases occurs among the most productive sector of the workforce.

After reaching the peak in 1999, at present, suicide rates in Thailand are in a decreasing phase. However, the outlook of suicides in Thailand is somewhat worrying. There are several socioeconomic trends that may lead the country into a difficult psychosocial situation. First, the rate of population growth is declining. This can affect the quantity and age structure of the population. The working age and aging population are likely to increase, whereas the proportion of children population aged 0–14 will tend to decrease. Second, females who become mothers have less time for their family as more of them begin to work outside the home. This will also make them more prone to outer stressors. Third, the family structure has changed. The household size has shrunk from an average of 5.6 persons per family in 1960 to 4.4 in 1990 (Wibulpolprasert et al. 2002). This may lead to less assistance and care among family members, particularly among the elderly who are more likely to be abandoned, resulting in higher negative impacts on elderly health. Finally, many Thais have become distant from religious practices. They are less restrictive in morality, more competitive, exploitative, self-centered, and power seeking.

The author agrees with Phillips et al. (2002) that developing countries need to develop novel strategies that are appropriate to their socioeconomic environments, rather than adopting programs developed from Western countries.

Suicide prevention efforts in Thailand should focus on controlling access to agricultural chemicals, providing high-risk individuals with alternative methods in dealing with stress during crisis, conducting research on the risk and protective factors and mechanisms operating in HIV/AIDS subjects with suicidal behavior, and improving the suicide monitoring system. A collaborative effort that brings together various disciplines to form an integrated intervention is important and necessary for moving the mission forward.

8

Singapore

Boon-Hock Chia and Audrey Chia

The suicide rate in Singapore has remained steady between 1993–2003, ranging from 8–12 per 100,000. The male: female suicide ratio is approximately 1.7:1 with jumping being the most common method of suicide. Ethnic Indians have the highest teenage suicide rate, whereas ethnic Chinese have a highest older adult rate. The ethnic Malay suicide rate is extremely low. Marriage has been shown to be a protective factor (especially in males) with the widowed or divorced being at higher risk. Life-stressors associated with suicide vary with age with relationship and study stress more predominant in the young, financial problems in the adult age-group, and physical illness in the old. Mental illness is diagnosed in 60% of suicide victims. Other risk and protective factors are discussed.

Introduction

Singapore is a small tropical country consisting of one main island and some 63 offshore islands located just 137 km north of the equator. It has a land area of 697.1 km2. The climate in Singapore is warm and humid all year round. There are two distinct monsoon seasons: the wet northeast monsoon season from December to March, and the dry southwest monsoon season from June to September.

In the early 1800s, Singapore was a small fishing village with fewer than 200 Malay fishermen. When Singapore became a British colony in the 1900s, it attracted a massive influx of economic immigrants from China and India. Following independence in 1965, it began to industrialize and modernize in order to survive economically. Singapore has a population density of 6,004 persons per square kilometer. Eighty-four percent of the population live in government subsidized high-rise flats.

Singapore is strategically located in South East Asia, and its population of 3.4 million residents is comprised mainly of Chinese (77%), Malay (14%), and Indian (8%). The different ethnic groups all have their own rich cultural heritage, religious beliefs and practices. Buddhism and Taoism (51%), Islam (15%), Christianity (15%), and Hinduism (4%) are the major religions practiced in Singapore.

Education is highly valued in Singapore. Every child in Singapore undergoes at least ten years of general education. A fundamental feature of Singapore's education system is its bilingual policy, which ensures that each child learns both English and his/her mother tongue so as to maintain an awareness of the individual's cultural heritage while learning the skills to function in a modern, industrialized economy. The general literacy rate (2003) is estimated to be 94.2%, and the level of education attained by the young is extremely high. The English-speaking workforce in Singapore is one of the best educated in the region. Most of the young are professionally or technically skilled. The unemployment rate in Singapore is low with a rate of 4.7% in 2003 (Leow, 2001).

Singapore has the third highest per capita income in Asia, after Brunei and Japan. It is politically and economically stable. Mobile phone subscribers number at 851 per 1,000 population. Sixty-five percent of homes are equipped with computers.

Its citizens enjoy a high level of health care. The life expectancy for residents stands at 76.9 years for males and 80.9 years for females. The police force is efficient and the crime rate relatively low.

However, life in Singapore can be stressful. For the country to remain successful, its citizens are expected to be diligent, resourceful, and able to respond and adapt quickly and efficiently to change. As a result, Singapore faces similar challenges in overcoming suicide as do many other modernized countries of the world.

Suicide in Singapore

Overall in Singapore, suicide is responsible for 2.4% of all deaths of the Chinese population, 2.6% of the Indian, and 0.6% of the Malays (Registry of Birth and Death 2004).

As expected, suicide is highly represented as a cause of death in the younger age group (Figure 1). In 2003, for example, suicide accounted for as much as 17% of deaths in people aged below 30 years. The higher rate in females reflects

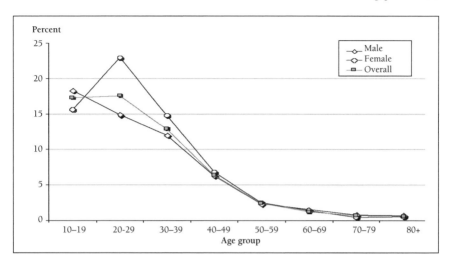

Figure 1　Percentage of deaths caused by suicide in Singapore, 2003.

the smaller number of accidental deaths in young females (as opposed to young males). Conversely, in the older age group, the proportion falls because of the increasing number of deaths by natural causes.

In Singapore, every case of unnatural death has to be investigated by the police. When investigating, the police have two main tasks: firstly, to gather information to exclude homicide, and, secondly, to help the coroners reach a verdict of cause — natural, misadventure, or suicide.

The investigation includes a careful examination of place of death, and collecting information from eyewitnesses and close relatives. Affidavits from relatives and friends are obtained, detailing the deceased personality, social situation, and behavior in the days prior to death. Physician and hospital reports are sought, and autopsy and toxicology examinations are undertaken.

All evidence is presented at the coroner's inquest, which normally is conducted three to six months after the death. A verdict of suicide is usually not made unless there is positive evidence of "suicide intent," or if there is "reasonable doubt." Doubtful cases are given an open verdict and assigned under the "undetermined category" in the Reports on Registration of Births and Deaths, Singapore. Between 2001 and 2003, for example, undetermined deaths accounted for 1.2% to 1.5% of total deaths in Singapore.

The suicide rates are underreported in Singapore, as they are in many other countries. One reason is that some suicides may be mistakenly placed under this undetermined category. Other factors that may influence the calculated rate include the way such deaths are investigated; the social pressure to deliver a result other than suicide; and the general attitude towards suicide in any particular society.

In Singapore, the "suicide to undetermined ratios" varied widely throughout the decades from 0.7:1 to 5.4:1 (Figure 2), with an average of 1.8:1 between 1980 and 2003. Changes in judiciary systems and coroners are thought to be the main determinant of the size of the undetermined rate at any one time. In a review of cases within the undetermined category, Chia (1978) estimated that up to 57% of such cases may indeed be "undeclared suicides." This being the case, the official suicide rate could be underreported by 13%.

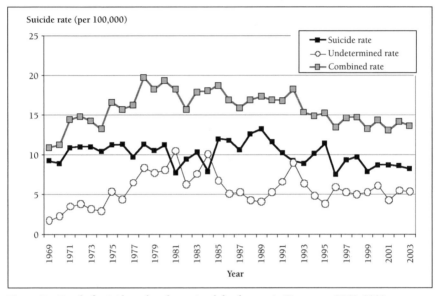

Figure 2   Trend of suicide and undetermined death rates in Singapore, 1969–2003.

In England and Wales, if every undetermined death were to be a misclassified suicide, the official suicide rate would underestimate the actual incidence of suicide by some 25% (Barraclough and Huges 1987). In Edinburgh, based on extensive record search, Overstone (1973) concluded that the Scottish Crown Counsel underreported suicide by 38%. In the USA, Toolan (1962) and Gist and Welsh (1989) postulated that the actual rates of suicide might exceed published rates by a factor of two or three. Thus, compared to other countries, the underreporting percentage in Singapore was low.

Suicide Trends

The suicide rate is calculated as the number of suicide per annum per 100,000 per population per annum. In Singapore, official suicide rates from 1968 to 2003 ranged between 8 and 12 per 100,000, with an average of 10 per 100,000 per annum.

In general, the official suicide rate in Singapore has remained relatively stable, with some decline since the late 1990s (Figure 2).

The question remains as to how accurate official rates are. Barraclough and Huges (1987) suggest that "The sum of the suicide rate and the undetermined rate may provide a better estimate of the true suicide rate than does the official suicide rate alone." (Page 96). Therefore, the combined rate may be a better indicator of true suicide rates.

Pertinently, this combined rate in Singapore coincides more closely to the periods of economic slowdown in Singapore than the official suicide curve. In Singapore, small increases in rates were noted, particularly during the Asian economic crises in 1985 and 1992. The general trend, however, remains downwards, suggesting that in Singapore, economic upheaval has, at most, a minor effect on the suicide rate. Also of note is the lack of appreciable increase in rate during the SARS (severe acute respiratory syndrome) epidemic in 2003.

Suicide is a desperate act, not often taken lightly. It is a reflection of general social stresses, individuals' ability to cope, and support mechanisms within family and social structures. Comparing suicide rates between countries provides one with a sense of the problem throughout the world. The manner in which suicide is classified or documented may grossly underestimate the rates in some countries. However, these rates offer one the opportunity to study differences and similarities in countries with different cultural mixes. In general, it appears that suicide rates are high in Eastern European nations, and low in Middle Eastern (Islamic) nations (Table 1). Variation in the male-female ratio also exists between East Asian and Western societies.

Table 1. Male and Female Suicide Rates (per 100,000) in Various Countries (WHO, 2003).

Country	Male					Female				
	Rate	15–24	35–44	55–64	75+	Rate	15–24	35–44	55–64	75+
Singapore (2000)	12.5	6.5	18.4	20.6	48.8	6.4	7.7	6.0	6.7	23.0
HK (1999)	16.7	9	16.8	23.7	53.1	9.8	6.8	9.9	12.6	38.4
China (1999)	13	5.4	12.6	23.1	84.2	6.4	8.6	13.9	20.7	61.2
Japan (1999)	36.5	16.5	37	65.9	60.7	14.1	7.3	10.5	19.5	34.1
India (1998)	12.1	na	na	na	na	9.1	na	na	na	na
Russia (2000)	74.1	48.8	110.5	109.5	109.3	11.9	9	14.3	18.9	32.0
USA (1992)	19.6	21.9	23.7	24.1	52.3	4.6	3.7	6.6	6.5	6.2
Australia (1999)	21.2	22.1	29.6	21.3	30.0	5.1	5.3	7.3	5.5	3.4
Iran (1991)	0.3	0.4	0.5	0.4	2	0.1	0.2	0.1	0.1	0

na: not available

Age and Gender Factors

Looking at the changing trends in Singaporean suicide rates of both males and females of different age groups (Figures 3a and 3b), we note the following:

1. The suicide rates are higher in older age groups.
2. Suicide rates in the older age group have fallen dramatically in males since the mid-1980s and continue to decline gradually in females.
3. Suicide rates in adults (aged 20–39 years) have remained relatively stable; they are higher in males (10–15:100,000) than in females (8:100,000).
4. Young male suicide rates have risen slowly over time.
5. Young female suicide rates have remained stable since the 1960s.
6. The male-female ratio is close to 1 in younger persons (< 20 years), with female rates being slightly higher than that of males.

One of the more striking features is the high rate of suicide among the older Singaporean population (Figure 3a). In the 1960s, the rates among males aged > 60 years exceeded 70:100,000. However, a steep decline has resulted in it falling to 30:100,000 in the early 2000s. Part of the reason for the high rates in the past was the high incidence of suicide among elderly single immigrant men who, looking for work, first entered Singapore at the turn of the century. These individuals had low monetary reserves and poor family ties in Singapore, and had lost touch with relations in their original countries. They were, in fact, "struck

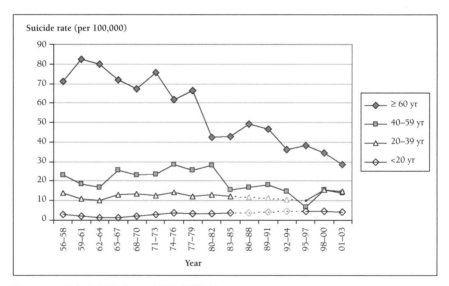

Figure 3a Male Suicide Rates, 1956–2003, Singapore.

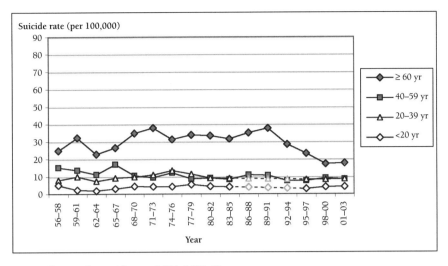

Figure 3b Female suicide rate, 1956–2003, Singapore.

in limbo"' and had little support when they became old, ill, and feeble (Chia 2001). Much of that generation has passed away. Most older individuals in Singapore now are second- or third-generation Singaporean; they are more financial able, better housed, have better access to health care, and are more likely to have family or community support networks. The rate of suicide still remains higher than that of other age groups but has gradually decreased over time.

Higher rates of suicide in the older age groups appear to occur in most societies (Table 1). The trend that has most worried the West, however, has been the high rates among young males. In Australia or the USA, for example, the rate within the 15–25 year age group is 20:100,000, which is about two times greater than in Singapore or China. In Asia, however, the female suicide rates are relatively higher. As a result, contrary to findings in most Western countries where there is a distinct predominance of male to female suicide in all age groups, the ratio among young Singaporeans is closer to one.

This relative female predominance in the young is also seen in other Asian countries, such as Hong Kong, Thailand, and India (Table 1; Zhang et al 2002; Aaron et al 2004; Yip 1998). In China, the young female rates (especially in rural areas) are extremely high. Low self-esteem, lack of education, increased subjugation, and low status of women within these societies is often blamed for this finding (Zhang et al 2002). Females who receive little support from relatives and the society may, when humiliated and rejected, think they have few options but to commit suicide. (Hassan 1983; Kok 1992)

In Singapore, however, suicide rates in young and middle-aged females (aged < 60 years) have remained very stable over the last three decades. Younger females, who are better educated with improved job prospects and greater financial independence, are better able to stand up to their parents or husbands if unfairly treated. This situation is far different from days of the past when females were subjugated; this should act as a protective factor. However, this new independence works both ways, for as females become more independent, they become exposed to a new set of risk factors, such as greater expectations, breakdown of family networks, and difficulties balancing home and work demands.

Looking at the suicide rates of both genders in different age groups (Figure 3), one sees that male rates start to become higher than females at age 20 and remain stable until age 50 at 15:100,000. These rates are lower than those in Western countries. However, from age 60 onwards, both male and female rates rise almost exponentially, exceeding that of the West (Figure 4, Table 1).

The high rate of suicide in the older Asian male has been well recognized (Tsoi and Kua 1987; Ko and Kua 1995). In China, male suicide rates are initially lower than that of females in the young, but they also "catch up" and then exceed female rates around age 55–64 (Zhang et al 2002).

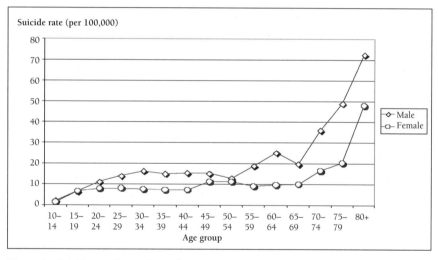

Figure 4   Suicide rates by gender and age group in Singapore, 2000–03.

Racial Differences

The presence of three distinct racial groups in Singapore, each with its own cultural and religious identity, offers an opportunity to study differences in suicide rates among groups.

In the first comprehensive study of suicide in Singapore, Murphy (1954) first noted that rates were extremely low in Malays and highest in Indians. A more recent survey of suicides in the years 2000–03 demonstrates that the Malay suicide rate still remains extremely low throughout all age groups (Figure 5). Indian suicide rates only slightly exceed Chinese rates in the younger age groups. In the older age groups, however, the Chinese suicide rates exceed those in all other ethnic groups. The suicide rate is especially high among older Chinese men. In 2003, the mean age of suicide in ethnic Chinese was 46 years compared to 34 years in Indians, and 29 years in Malays (Report on Registration of Birth and Deaths 2004). In the years 2000–03, the overall suicide rates in ethnic Chinese, Indian, and Malay were 14.1, 13.3, and 3 per 100,000, respectively.

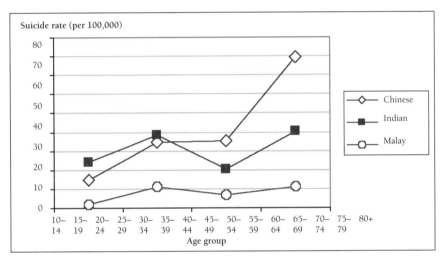

Figure 5a Male suicide rate by age and race, 2000–03.

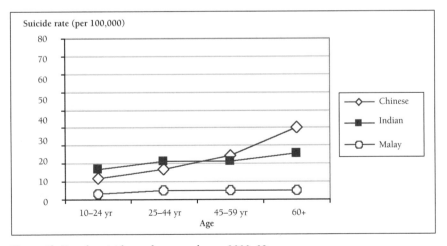

Figure 5b Female suicide rate by age and race, 2000–03.

The Chinese male who was brought up in the 1940—1960s had two main priorities: be filial to parents and provide financial support to the family. The male role was to spend long hours working and providing for the family. His mother and wife were responsible for care of the home and his off-springs. This was at a time when Singaporeans were encouraged to have smaller (two children) families. With a changing society, an older man may now find himself distant from his family upon retirement. His grown children are likely to be more economically independent and more likely to set up smaller family units of their own. Less respect and deference is accorded him (as parent or grandparent), as it would have been in the past. Retirement may bring with it a loss of income, sense of self-worth, and face. With increasing infirmity, the older individual may be frustrated at the social and economic burden he places on his family, and be too ashamed to ask his children for help. Suicide may be seen as a noble sacrifice for the good of the family. A common phrase used among the older Chinese is "I'm old and useless; not to be a burden, might as well be dead;" it is often said with a wry resigned smile on their faces.

The pattern of suicide in different age groups in ethnic Indians varies slightly. The rates in the young (< 45 years) are higher than in the Chinese, but the trend is reverse in the elderly. In the Indian culture, young females are expected to be passive, docile, and nonassertive; they are often downtrodden, devalued, and considered burdensome (Hassan 1983; Mehta 1990). When provoked by the unreasonable expectations of their parents, their husbands or in-laws, they are less likely to be supported by their family or their society (Kakar 1978). Marriages are arranged and approved by elders in the family, resulting in much stress and humiliation for the young Indian females who are rejected. Young Indian females may feel that they have no recourse but to use suicide as a means of receiving freedom from emotional pain and suffering. The young Indian male, on the other hand, enjoys a privileged position in the household. However, in return, there is greater pressure on the Indian male to comply with parental wishes, live up to role expectations, take over the family business, and succeed and excel in life (Purushotam 2004). These stressors may be multiplied in societies where Indians are an ethnic minority.

Interestingly, the Singaporean Indian suicide rates dip and remain stable in the older age groups. A similar trend is noted among the elderly in the Indian subcontinent, where rates also are low. This is contrary to the general worldwide trend of increasing rates with age. Several factors may contribute to this phenomenon. The average age expectancy in the subcontinent is much lower than that in Western countries. At the same time, the elderly, traditionally, are well respected and continue to be looked after by their families after retirement. They continue to play an active role in the family, and their opinions are always sought in important matters (Khan 2002). It is possible that some of these protective factors are carried over into the Singaporean Indian population.

The Malays in Singapore have the lowest suicide rates for both genders. The rate of 3:100,000 is low by world standards. It would be tempting to assume that the rate has been underestimated. However, given the detailed and thorough nature through which deaths are classified in Singapore, gross underreporting is unlikely. The probable explanation may lie in the Malays' tradition and religion (Maaruf 2004). Being indigenous to the land, they enjoy stability in a long-established society, which helps "moderate and cushion the impact of change." (Page 208–28). The Malay family structure is large, extended, and close-knit. While family size in Chinese and Indian families have been decreasing over time, the size of the Malay family has remained high (Leow 2001). Central to their culture is their religious (spiritual) approach to life. Materialistic needs are less important. Life becomes less complicated and relatively free of personal conflict and burden. Their religion (Islam) states categorically that life is the most valuable gift humans possess; suicide is forbidden. Their practice of fasting every year for one month strengthens their faith and increases their tolerance for physical discomfort. The rates of suicide in Malays in Kuala Lumpur (Malaysia), many Middle Eastern countries (such as Iran, Bahrain, Egypt), and Muslims in India, have been estimated at 1:100,000, 0.1–0.4:100,000, and 0.46:100,000, respectively (WHO 2003).

The Malay custom also considers women the weaker sex but support is provided when women are in need. For example, it is entirely acceptable for women to become divorced from their husbands without shame. This frees them from the necessity of hiding an unhappy marriage for the benefit of relatives or the public, and frees them from unnecessary misery and constraint. Divorce rates in ethnic Malays are one of the highest in Singapore.

Marital Status

Since the seminal study by Durkheim (1897), many studies have recognized the protective power of marriage against suicide (Lloyd and Yip 2001; Yip and Thorburn 2004; Stack 2000; Smith Mercy and Conn 1988; Danigelis and Pope 1969). The protective power of marriage would be more obvious to males than females (Lloyd and Yip 2001; Stack 2000). Kok and Aw (1992), in their study of all cases of suicide occurring in the year 1986 in Singapore, found that the married subject had the lowest rate of 13.2, rising to 17.5 in the single, 31.0 in the divorced, and 42.2 in the widowed.

If marriage has protective power, then the married-single ratio should be less than 1. From Singapore data collected between 1995 and 2003 (Table 2), several observations can be made:

1. Marriage was not protective in young people (aged < 25 years) of both genders and may even be a provoking factor in this group.
2. Marriage appeared to be more protective in males than females. This effect was most obvious in males aged > 25 years, and females aged between 25 and 59 years.
3. Marriage was not protective in older females (aged > 60years).
4. Young widowed females (aged 10–24 years) had the highest suicide rate (68.9).
5. Widowed and divorced subsets had higher suicide rates than the combined single and married group.

Table 2. Suicide Rate by Gender, Age, and Marital Status, 1995–2003, Singapore.

	Single	Married	Divorced/ Separated	Widowed	Married : Single ratio
Male					
10–24	6.8	13.1	–	–	1.9:1
25–59	31.9	9.4	6.3	43.1	0.3:1
60+	76.5	33.6	31.3	24.5	0.4:1
Overall	17.0	13.5	28.9	16.5	0.8:1
Female					
10–24	4.8	11.8	–	68.9	2.5:1
25–59	12.5	6.6	6.3	23.8	0.5:1
60+	21.8	22.4	16.3	21.4	1.1:1
Overall	7.6	8.5	14.1	24.1	1.1:1

Employment Status

Unemployment, with all its social implications, is a major risk factor for suicide. The correlation between unemployment and suicide rates has been demonstrated in some countries (Boor 1980). The percentage of unemployment among suicide victims in Singapore is 49.3% and is comparable to the 50% quoted in other studies. This strong association with unemployment in Singapore was also noted by Murphy (1954).

From Table 3, it can be noted that the suicide rates for the unemployed was extremely high (59.3) — about nine times that of the employed (6.8).

The high rate of suicide among the unemployed reflects the heavy burden of unemployment in many societies. In Singapore, no social security system exists. Charity organizations cater to the very poor and very sick. The able-bodied unemployed, however, may find it necessary to rely on their savings or on the generosity of family and friends. The social stigma, coupled with stress of an older person trying to find a job quickly while supporting a household, may be enormous.

Table 3. Suicide Rate (per 100,000) by Occupation, 2000–03.

	Male	Female	Overall
Occupation			
Economic Active			
Employed	7.9	4.5	6.8
Unemployed	66.0*	51.4*	59.3*
Economic Inactive			
Student	8.7	5.9	7.4
Homemaker	–	4.3	4.3
Retired	21.0	12.7	16.9

* Age 15–55 years

Other Factors Associated with Suicide

As we have seen, the suicide rates in Singapore vary according to gender, age, and race. However, the precipitating or ongoing factors within these groups may vary. Factors associated with suicide include life stressors, mental or physical illnesses, presence of abnormal personality traits, and substance and alcohol abuse (Chia and Tsoi 1972).

The study of these factors is often done retrospectively through a detailed review of the events surrounding and preceding the event. In Singapore, these details are obtained secondhand from affidavits of relatives and friends filed in Coroner Court records. Table 4 summarizes the factors present in the 1,356 suicides occurring between 2000–03.

Life stressors together with mental disorders are leading risk factors, except in the older group, where physical illness is the prominent risk factor. Often, multiple factors may interact.

Life Stressors

Relationship problems (between boy-girl, husband-wife, parent-child, relatives, or friends) figure highly in all subgroups. These include conflict and disagreement, unrequited love, bereavement, or loss, and may originate at home, school, or work. In females, relationship problems are the main life-stressor, while in males, these rank directly after job/financial problems.

Social factors vary in different age groups. In the young, it may include the pressures of study, examinations, or national (military) service. In the elderly, social problems range from loneliness and the sense of being a burden or feeling unwanted to having difficulty paying for health care or finding suitable accommodation.

Table 4. **Factors Associated with Suicide in Singapore, 2000–03.**

	Gender		Age			Race		
	Male (n=845) %	Female (n=511) %	Young (n=155) %	Adult (n=856) %	Old (n=345) %	Chinese (n=1,201) %	Indian (n=105) %	Malay (n=105) %
Life Stressors	66	62	81	70	45	64	70	80
Relationship	28	43	52	35	20	n.a.	n.a.	n.a.
Job/finance	40	24	17	27	10	n.a.	n.a.	n.a.
Social	16	16	27	10	26	n.a.	n.a.	n.a.
Legal	12	4	7	13	2	n.a.	n.a.	n.a.
Substance abuse	21	10	17	18	7			
Illegal drug abuse	14	7	n.a.	n.a.	n.a.	12	9	14
Alcohol abuse	7	3	n.a.	n.a.	n.a.	4	16	2
Habitual gambler	6	2	n.a.	n.a.	n.a.	5	1	2
Personality traits	18	6	25	18	9	16	27	16
Mental disorder	53	70	43	66	51	60	50	58
Physical illness	38	40	15	4	78	40	27	27

Note: n.a. — not available

Alcohol and Substance Abuse

Unlike in Western countries, alcoholism and substance abuse are not major risk factors in Singapore. Illegal drug abuse is found in 10% of suicides in all ethnic groups, while alcoholism is more common in Indians. Another form of addiction, pathological gambling, is an occasional problem seen especially in the Chinese population.

Mental Illness

In reviewing suicides between 2000 and 2003, mental illnesses were diagnosed in 60% of suicide victims (Table 5). Schizophrenia was the most common major psychotic illness diagnosed (14.2%), followed by major depression (4.8%). Minor depressive disorder, however, was noted in 29.4%. Psychiatric drugs were detectable in the blood of 34% of the suicide victims at autopsy.

The percentage of major depressive disorder found associated with suicide is probably markedly underreported in this study. Many suicide victims who were diagnosed with minor depressive disorder were probably suffering from major depressive disorder.

Schizophrenia is the major mental illness most commonly associated with suicide in Singapore. This differs from the West where suicide is often associated

Table 5. Type of Mental Illness Associated with Suicide in Singapore, 2000–03.

Types	No (% total) (n=1,356)
Major Mental Disorder:	
Schizophrenia	193 (14.2%)
Psychosis, paranoia, morbid jealousy	85 (6.2%)
Major depressive disorder	66 (4.8%)
Dementia	11 (0.8%)
Minor Mental Disorder:	
Minor depressive disorder	400 (29.4%)
Stress reaction, adjustment disorder, post-traumatic stress	17 (1.3%)
Obsessive-compulsive disorder	5 (0.3%)
Panic/phobias	3 (0.2%)
Total	780 (59.1%)

with major depression. It also differs from mental-hospital-based studies in Singapore, where the percentage of schizophrenia has been estimated at 78%–84% (Tsoi and Chia 1974; Kua and Sim 1982). These figures highlight the higher risk of suicide in mentally ill patients, especially when they have been recently hospitalized.

Of the Singaporean suicide victims (2000–03), 39% had contact with mental health service one month prior to their suicide, and 43% had contact one year prior to suicide. Of these, 29% had past admission to a mental hospital or a psychiatric unit in a general hospital, 4.5% had consulted private psychiatrists, 2% had been treated in a psychiatric outpatient department, and 0.7% had other psychiatric treatment.

The percentages of persons who had contact with mental health or medical services, however, will vary with the availability of such services. In Western countries, an estimated one-third of suicide victims had contact with mental health services within one year, and 20% within one month prior to suicide (Luoma et al. 2002). In China, where services are poorer, the percentage of those having had contact with mental health services was as low as 9% (Phillips et al 2002).

Physical Illness

Kok and Aw (1992), in a study of Singapore suicide victims in the year 1986, found that physical illness or pain was associated with suicide in 57% of cases. A recent review (2000–03) suggests that significant physical illness was present in 41.6%.

In Singapore from 2000–03, illnesses commonly associated with suicide included those causing severe pain or discomfort such as myocardial infarct (15.7%), gastric ulcer (8.8%), and arthritis (8.1%); difficulty in breathing such as chronic respiratory disease (15.4%); terminal or incurable diseases such as cancer (14.8%) or HIV/AIDS; and those causing impaired motility such as a stroke (10.8%) or visual impairment (7.8%).

When interviewed, many relatives reported the victim as having been "depressed" at the time of death.

Physical illness and functional impairment increases the suicide risk (Yeates, Duberstein, and Caine 2005). This process appears to be mediated by depression. However, more work still needs to define more precisely the interactions between emotional, physical, and social factors that determine risk for suicide in the older adult.

Communication of Intent

Verbal Warnings, Pre-suicidal Planning and Behavioral Change Prior to Suicide

After a suicide has occurred, the question arises whether there was any warning issued prior to the event that may have alerted doctors and relatives.

Verbal warnings consist of expressions that life has no meaning, of suicide intent, a suicidal threat, or bidding farewell. Pre-suicidal planning involves tidying up one's affairs (e.g., finalizing a will, expressing concern, or leaving instructions to loved ones who are left behind). Behavior changes, such as a sudden calm or euphoria, excessive spending, generous gift giving, sudden withdrawal, or refusal to eat, may occur days to weeks before the suicide event.

In the years 2000–03, verbal warning was received in almost half of all suicides (Table 6). In most of these cases, there was some expression of suicide intent (34%). Younger subjects were more likely to issue a verbal threat (e.g., "If you do not do X, I will kill myself") than older individuals.

Pre-suicide planning and behavior change was noticed in only a small percentage (< 11%). A higher proportion of young suicides were more likely to leave a note behind. In some cases, they would send a text message (SMS) or make a phone call just prior to the event.

Suicide Notes

Suicide notes offer a window into the thoughts and feelings that encompass the suicide act (Chia et al. 2008). They are valuable documents and furnish important

Table 6 Communication Prior to Suicide by Age in Singapore, 2000–03.

	Young (n=155) (age 10–24 years)	No. (% of total) Adult (n=856) (age 25–59 years)	Old (n=345) (age 60+ years)
Verbal warning*	66 (42.5%)	346 (40.4%)	182 (52.7%)
. Life has no meaning	11 (7%)	49 (5.7%)	40 (11.5%)
. Suicide intent	54 (34.8%)	299 (34.9%)	154 (44.6%)
. Suicide threat	10 (6.4%)	32 (3.7%)	7 (2%)
. Farewell	6 (3.8%)	8 (0.9%)	1 (0.2%)
Pre-suicide planning	14 (9%)	92 (10.7%)	31 (8.9%)
Behavioral change	10 (6.4%)	42 (4.9%)	9 (2.6%)
Note, SMS, phone	74 (47.7%)	221 (25.8%)	38 (11%)
Past suicide attempt	32 (20.6%)	215 (25.1%)	65 (18.8%)

* Each individual may express more than one sort of verbal warning

data that will help in the understanding of the suicide. In some cases, the notes help the family understand why the suicide has occurred; they have a therapeutic role.

The main reasons why people leave suicide notes were to:
1. Explain why they had to kill themselves (69%)
2. Express their deep emotions, both negative (69%) and positive (62%)
3. Leave behind requests (40.5), advice (27.6%), information (27.6%), and instructions (22.6%) (e.g., how the body is to be deposed and what type of funeral to have)
4. Ask forgiveness
5. Bid their relatives or friends a final farewell
6. Exculpate or free others from blame

Mode of Suicide

The mode of suicide is usually determined by what is available to the person at any one time. In rural areas, pesticide ingestion and hanging are more popular. In areas where there is a strong gun culture, shooting oneself is more common.

In Singapore, the method of suicide has changed drastically during the last 40 years. In the early years, hanging and poisoning were the major methods used. However, with the construction of more high-rise dwellings since the 1970s, jumping is now the most common mode of death, followed by hanging, poisoning, and gas (Table 7).

Almost 94% of Singapore's population currently resides in high-rise flats. Jumping is easily available and eminently affordable. It is believed to be quick and painless and, unfortunately, also provides little opportunity for rescue and for changing one's mind.

Table 7. Trend of Suicide Rates (per 100,000) by Method in Singapore.

	1940–44	1960–64	1980–84	2000–04
Jumping	0.3	1.5	6.0	7.8
Hanging	10.4	4.0	2.4	1.8
Drowniing	0.7	1.0	0.2	0.1
Poisoning	3.5	1.4	0.8	0.4
Gas	–	–	0.1	0.3
Shooting	0.2	0.1	–	–
Knife	0.9	0.2	0.1	0.1
Other	0.1	0.2	0.3	0.2
Total	16.1	8.3	10.0	10.6

Interestingly, in Hawaii, it was found that the Chinese were more likely to jump from high-rise buildings (48.7%) than other ethnic groups (Tseng et al 1992). In Hong Kong, jumping has become increasingly common and replaced other methods of suicide. In Singapore, a greater percentage of Chinese jump than do Malays or Indians. Thus, it would appear that Chinese, as a race, may prefer to commit suicide by jumping from high-rise buildings.

However, death by inhaling carbon monoxide from burning charcoal, a relatively new mode of death, has become increasing popular in Hong Kong. One such case was noted in Singapore in 2003, and four in 2004. All subjects were Chinese with ages ranging between 24 and 45 years. They were a computer savvy group and may have learned of this method through the Internet.

Timing of Suicide

Suicides in temperate countries have been found to fluctuate with the seasons, increasing in the spring months. In tropical countries, however, no seasonal pattern appears to exist (Ting and Tan 1969; Parker, Gao, and Machin 2001). Recent data, from the 2000–03 review of suicide, also demonstrated very little differences throughout the year, although numbers were slightly lower in the months of October to December. There was no preference for any particular day of the week. Specific holidays, such as Chinese New Year, which previously appeared protective (Ho 1985), no longer seems so. Suicide in Singapore, however, seems extremely low during the country's National Day. Only three cases of suicide were noted on that day over the last ten years (i.e., 0.30 per day, compared to an average of 0.75 per day in the week prior and after). National Day is an important day for Singaporeans; there is a great collective celebration of community solidarity, unity, and progress, culminating in a grand parade and a pledge of loyalty to the country by the citizens.

Suicide Prevention in Singapore

Suicide is a desperate final act by individuals to whom life seems so hopeless and bleak that they take their own lives. It is, indirectly, a sad reflection of a society's failure to recognize the predicaments of individuals within its midst and its inability to render the necessary assistance. Each society is unique. It is through the study of suicide risk factors that one better understands the specific problems prevalent within the society.

In Singapore, the problems are complex. People of different ages, gender, and race have their own sets of problems. The risk is highest in older Chinese males, in the younger Indian males and females, and in those who are widowed /divorced, and unemployed. In the young, relationships and social factors, such as study stresses, are major risk factors; in mid-age adults, job/financial problems and mental illness are important, and in the older age group, physical illness is most significant. Those with mental illness (especially with schizophrenia and depressive disorders) are also at particular risk, especially if they have been recently hospitalized.

The first step in prevention is to recognize that a problem exists. The next is to raise public awareness of this problem and to develop specific programs to tackle them. In the young, for example, the emphasis may be the fostering of better relationships between parent and child; developing social skills and coping mechanisms; moderating the expectations of education excellence; providing counseling centers where young people can go to seek help; and easing the trauma of entry into national service training. The working adult may benefit from education in finance management; financial advisory services for those with a sudden cash-flow problem; better job recruitment or skills re-training programs; and support groups for those with drug, alcohol, or gambling problems. For the elderly, there should be an effort to seek out those that require help; to provide good affordable health care; to increase awareness of the psychological needs of the elderly; and to set up community support networks within the society.

In terms of the management of mental health, there needs to be a greater awareness of the problem within the medical profession. The general practitioner must be able to identify the patient at risk. The psychiatrist must be able to accurately diagnose the mental condition present and provide adequate treatment. In some difficult recalcitrant cases, aggressive treatment may be necessary. There are now new and more effective medications to treat many mental disorders with fewer side effects. Inappropriate suboptimal therapy or poor patient compliance are common factors in patient relapse, which, in turn, increases suicide risk. Social and community networks must be set up to aid these patients and their families on discharge.

Prevention of suicide is a public health issue (Singh and Jenkins 2000). Suicide not only destroys a life but also has repercussion throughout society (via family, friends, and physicians) left in its wake. However, it will be foolhardy to think that we can cure all the ills of society. There is a common Buddhist saying, "To live is to suffer."' There will always be factors (illness, bereavement, economic recessions, natural disasters, and wars) that are totally out of our control. How we fare, however, depends on our coping skills, our social support network, and our medical and mental health services, which we must utilize effectively to alleviate suffering (both mentally and physically).

9

India

Lakshmi Vijayakumar

Over 100,000 persons die by suicide in India every year. The suicide rate —
increased by 64% from 6.4 per 100,000 in 1982 to 10.5 per 100,000 in 2002. The
male-female ratio is consistently low at 1.5 to 1. About 38% of suicides in India
are committed by persons below 30 years of age. Poisoning, hanging, and self-
immolation (setting fire to oneself) were the common methods used to commit
suicide. The crucial and causal role of depression in suicide has limited validity
in India, whereas alcoholism emerges as a significant risk factor. Less than 10%
of persons who had committed suicide had ever seen a mental health professional.
Family problems and illness each contribute to 23% of suicides. Conflicts related
to marriage, such as dowry disputes, arranged marriages, and love failures, are
significant environmental stressors. About 1% of suicides in India are suicide
pacts. The different risk and protective factors and the scarcity of human and
economic resources necessitate the development of a national suicide prevention
plan for India that is cost effective and culturally sensitive.

Introduction

India is an ancient country with diverse economic, social, cultural, and religious
dimensions. Suicide in India is intrinsically intertwined with the history of India
and its varying beliefs and philosophies. Ancient scriptures termed suicide as
"atmagathaka." The earliest known scriptures are Vedas, which contains verses
suggestive of suicide. The Upanishads, which are considered as Hindu philosophy
distilled, condemn suicide. Although the scriptures do not support suicide, there

are numerous instances in epics, like Ramayana and Mahabharatha, where suicide had been glorified. In Dharmasasthra (book of moral code and conduct), there exists a separate chapter titled "Allowable Suicides." The practices of suttee (widow self-immolation) and jauhar (immolation of every female in the family and/or tribe to escape the invaders) were prevalent in India (Thakur 1963). Individual suicides were condemned, but religious suicides were condoned.

Data and Method

In India, it is the police who classify all unnatural deaths (Cr Act 174) into suicides, accidents, and unidentified deaths. Homicides are registered in a different act. The police come to the conclusion based on their investigation and post mortem report. In addition, the verdict of suicide should also be passed by panchayatdars, who are prominent citizens of the locality, and by the neighbors, before the police can classify a death as suicide. In the case of death of a woman who has been married for less than seven years, the police, after registering the case, will transfer it to the local magistrate for the final verdict of death. This was promulgated to combat the menace of dowry deaths. The suicide statistics are published every year by the National Crime Research Bureau, Ministry of Home Affairs, Government of India.

There is general consensus among experts that inefficient civil registration systems, variation in certification, social stigma, religious sanctions, and legal issues lead to underreporting of suicide in India. A study in Vellore has found that the actual number of suicides is nine times more than the official figures (Joseph et al. 2003). Data on suicide is available from 1967 from the Ministry of Home Affairs.

Results

Suicide Rates

Over 100,000 people commit suicide every year in India. It can be seen from Figure 1 that there was a small decline in the suicide rate from 1975 to 1986 and a steady increase thereafter. The suicide rate increased by 43.5% from 6.2 in 1980 to 8.9 in 1990, and by 21.3% from 1990 to 10.8 in 2000.

The suicide rate increased by 64% from 6.4 in 1982 to 10.5 in 2002. The suicide rate of men increased by 70% from 7.3 to 12.8, and the rate of women by 52% from 5.4 to 8.2. Since the year 2000 the suicide rate has stabilized and there is the suggestion of a slight decline over the period 2001–2003.

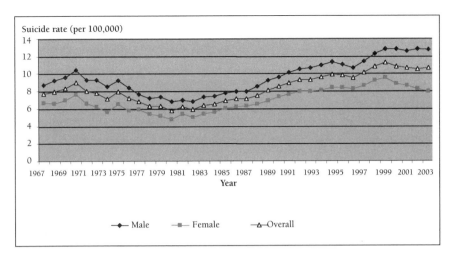

Figure 1. Suicide rates in India, 1967–2003.

There is wide variation in the suicide rate within the country. Kerala, Karnataka, Tamil Nadu, and Andhra Pradesh, which are the southern states in India, have a suicide rate of more than 15 per 100,000. In the northern states of Bihar, Madhya Pradesh, Uttar Pradesh, and Rajasthan, the suicide rate is less than 5 per 100,000. This variable pattern has been persistent during the last 20 years.from 1983. Higher literacy rate, a better reporting system, lower external aggressive behavior, higher socioeconomic status, and higher expectations are possible explanatory variables for this unique distribution of suicide in India.

Age and Gender

The suicide rate of women is lower than that of men, but by a small margin when compared to the global gender ratio for suicide. The male-female ratio has been consistently low at 1.5 to 1.

The majority of suicides in India occur at a younger age compared to developed countries. Figure 2 shows that girls outnumber boys below 14 years. Between the ages of 18 years and29 years, almost equal numbers of men and women commit suicide. It is obvious that in India young women below 30 years are at a higher risk of committing suicide (Mayer and Ziaian 2002); a total of 38.2% of suicides are committed by people below the age of 30, and 34% are in the age group of 30–44 years. The fact that 72% of suicides in India are committed by persons below the age of 44 years suggests the imposition of a huge social, emotional, and economic burden on the society.

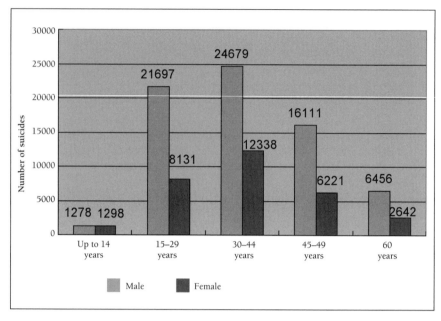

Figure 2   Suicides by gender and age distribution, 2003, India.

Marital Status

In the field of suicidology, it has often been discussed that being single, widowed, or divorced is a risk factor for suicide, and that being married acts as a protective factor. There is less evidence that marital status is a significant risk factor for suicide in studies conducted in developing countries (Vijayakumar 2005a). A study in India concluded that marital status alone was not predictive of suicide (Rao 1991). In 2002, 68.2% of persons who committed suicide were married, while 22% were unmarried. Divorced and separated constituted about 4% and widows 5.8%.

Rural Versus Urban

There appears to be no difference in the suicide rate in rural and urban areas of India. In 2002, the suicide rate of union territories was 10.51; the suicide rate of the urban areas (35 cities) 10.5; and the national rate 10.5 (National Crime Research Bureau 2002).

Method Used

The Government of India Suicide Data for the year 2003 reveals that poisoning (37.1%), hanging (28.4%), and self-immolation (9.7%) were the most common methods used to commit suicide. Pesticides were used by 19.4% of those taking poison. Self- immolation was used by 10,655 persons and is the only method where women outnumber men; a total of 67% of self-immolations are by women. Those who survive this horrific method are often left with permanent disfigurement. The Hindu concept of fire as a purifier, the practices of sati and jauhar, which were prevalent two centuries ago, and the easy accessibility of kerosene at home are likely to be the reasons for the prevalence of self-immolation in India.

Mental Disorders

Two case-controlled studies using the psychological autopsy technique have been conducted in India, one in Chennai (Vijayakumar and Rajkumar 1999) and one in Bangalore (Gururaj, Isaac, Subhakrishna and Ranjani 2004). Among those who have committed suicide, mental disorders were found in 88% of completers in Chennai. Only 43% of completers were found to have mental disorders in the Bangalore study. This low prevalence in Bangalore could be due to the fact that an overall attempt was made to identify the presence or absence of mental disorders, and no psychiatric or diagnostic evaluations were made.

Even though more than 60% of the depressive's suicides had only mild-to-moderate depression, countless experts have found that affective disorders are the most important diagnosis related to suicide. In a case-controlled psychological autopsy study in Chennai (Vijayakumar and Rajkumar 1999), mood disorders were found only in 25% of completed suicides, and when adjustment disorder with depressed mood was included, it was 35%. The crucial and causal role of depression in suicide has limited validity in India. Even those who were depressed for a short duration and had only mild-to-moderate symptoms. The majority committed suicide in their very first episode of depression.

Although social drinking is not a way of life in India, alcoholism plays a significant role in suicide. Around 30%–50% of males were under the influence of alcohol at the time they committed suicide, and many wives have been driven to suicide by their alcoholic husbands. Not only has there been a large number of alcoholic suicides, but many came from alcoholic families and who then became heavily dependant on alcohol after early consumption in life. The odds ratio (OR) for alcoholism was 8.25 (confidence interval [CI] 2.9–3.2) in Chennai (Vijayakumar and Rajkumar 1999) and 4.49 (CI 2.0–6.8) in Bangalore (Gururaj et al. 2004).

About 8% of suicides in India are committed by persons suffering from schizophrenia. Srinivasan and Thara found that the male-female ratio for schizophrenic suicide is more or less equal (Srinivasan and Thara 2003). According to the government report, only 4.74% of suicides in the country are due to mental disorders. Although diagnosable mental disorders were found in 88% of suicides in the Chennai study, only 10% had ever seen a mental health professional.

Personality disorder was found in 20% of completed suicides. The OR was 9.5 (CI 2.29–84.11). Cluster B personality disorder was found in 12% of suicides. Comorbid diagnosis was found only in 30% of suicides.

A history of previous suicide attempts increases the risk of subsequent suicides. The OR for previous suicide attempts was 5.2 (CI 1.96–17.34) in Chennai and 42.62 (CI 5.78–313.88) in Bangalore. In the Bangalore study, a family history of completed suicide had a greater risk (OR 7.69; CI 2.13–32.99) compared with a family history of attempted suicide. In the Chennai study, 12% had a family history of suicide (OR 1.33; CI 0.6–3.09) in first-degree relatives and 18% in second-degree relatives (Fisher's Exact Test p< 0.001).

Environmental Factors

Environmental factors have always been associated with suicide. Figure 3 shows that, according to official data, "Not known" and "Other causes" total approximately 40% of causes for suicide. Among the specified causes, "Illness" and "Family problems" were the major ones at approximately 23% each.

Hegde, in his study of 51 suicides, found that 37% had family problems (Hegde 1980). A study from Manipal revealed that marital difficulties and conflicts with key family members were seen in the majority of those attempting suicide (Latha, Bhat, and D'Souza 1996).

Domestic violence is a fairly common occurrence, and its practice is, to a large extent, socially and culturally condoned in India. In a population-based study on domestic violence, 9,938 women were studied in different parts of the country and across various sections of the society. It was found that 40% had experienced domestic violence (Kumar et al. 2005), and 64% had shown a significant correlation between domestic violence and suicidal ideation (WHO 2001). The Bangalore study found that domestic violence was found in 36% of suicides and was a major risk factor (OR 6.82; CI 4.02–11.94) (Gururaj et al. 2004).

Another distinctive form of abuse in Indian society is associated with dowry disputes. In India, dowries are a continuing series of gifts endowed before or after marriage. When dowry expectations are not met, the young bride is harassed, and many suicides occur by self-immolation. In the year 2002, 2,410 (male 32; female 2,378) suicides in India were due to dowry-related issues and constituted 2.2% of all suicides. (National Crime Records Bureau 2002)

About 50%–60% of marriages in India are arranged by families. Young persons who love each other, but whose families disapprove of their relationship, commit suicide, either together or alone, as the prospect of marrying each other means defying and severing ties with the family. Sometimes unrequited love is also the reason for adolescent suicides. Around 3% of suicides in India are due to love failures. (National Crime Records Bureau 2002)

In the year 2002, the proportion of women committing suicide were as follows: dowry disputes (98.7%), divorce (75.6%), Not having children (71%), Physical abuse (59.3%), cancellation or non-settlement of marriage (58.6%), extra marital relationship (58.5%), and illegitimate pregnancy (97%). Eight men committed suicide because they had been responsible for an illegitimate pregnancy.

It can be seen that conflicts related to marriage play a crucial role in suicide, particularly in women, in India.

A distressing feature in India is the frequent occurrence of suicide pacts and family suicides. A suicide pact is a mutual arrangement between two or more people to die together at the same time and usually in the same place. Family suicides can be suicide pacts or suicide/homicide e.g., wherein the adults murder their children prior to their own suicide. In a study in India, 148 pacts involving 324 persons were studied. Women (55.7%) outnumbered men (44.3%) (X^2 29.7; p < 0001). Pacts involving extramarital partners or lovers (39.8%) were more common than pacts with spouses (26.9%) (Vijayakumar and Thilothammal 1993). In the year 2002, 1,035 persons died in suicide pacts, which involved 233 children (male 112; female 121). Thus, suicide pacts are due primarily to social reasons and can be viewed as a form of protest against societal norms and expectations.

Poverty, unemployment and economic problems account for 6.6% of suicides in India (Figure 3). The recent spate of suicides in the Warangal district of Andhra Pradesh in southern India was directly attributed to losses incurred when cotton crops failed (Stone 2002).

Education problems, especially among students in the adolescent age group, increased the risk of suicide fourfold (OR 4.33; CI 2.73–6.86) (Stone 2002). About 2% (n = 2,250) of suicides in India are committed following failure in exams. Enormous competition to get into colleges, the media hype associated with results, and the shame associated with failure pushes the distressed adolescent to suicide.

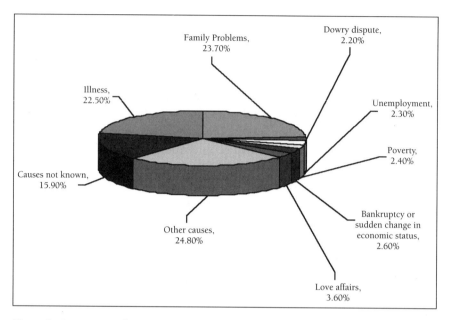

Figure 3   Percentages of various causes of suicide, 2003, India.

Clusters of Suicides

The media sometimes give intense publicity to "suicide clusters" — a series of suicides that occur, mainly among young people, in a small area within a short period of time. These have a contagious effect, especially when they have been glamorized, provoking imitation or "copycat suicides." This phenomenon has been observed in India on many occasions, especially after the death of a celebrity, most often a movie star or a politician. The wide exposure given to these suicides in the media has lead to suicides in a similar manner. Copying methods shown in movies are also not uncommon. This is a serious problem, especially in India where film stars enjoy an iconic status and wield enormous influence, especially over the young who often look up to them as role models. In 1990, the Government of India implemented the recommendation of the Mandal Commission to reserve 27% of the positions for employment in the government from the underprivileged class as a form of affirmative action for improving their status. It created unrest in the student community, and a student committed self-immolation in front of a group of people, protesting against such a reservation. This was sensationalized and widely publicized in the media. There was a spate of student self-immolations (n = 31) throughout the country. These copycat suicides caused a public outcry and was considered one of the reasons for the fall of the government at the time. (Vijayakumar 2004).

Social Change

The effects of modernization, specifically in India have lead to sweeping changes in the socioeconomic, sociophilosophical, and cultural arenas of an individual's life and are greatly adding to the tensions in life leading to substantially higher rates of suicide (Gehlot and Nathawat 1983).

In India, the high rate of suicide among young adults can be associated with greater socioeconomic stressors that have followed the liberalization of the economy and privatization leading to the loss of job security, huge disparities in incomes, and the inability to meet role obligations in the new socially changed environment. The breakdown of the joint family system that had previously provided emotional support and stability is also seen as an important factor (De Leo 2003).

Religiosity

Religion acts as a protective factor both at the individual and societal level. The often-debated question is whether the social network offered by the religion is protective or whether a person's individual faith is protective. The major religion in India is Hinduism. The duties of the priest are solely within the temple, and there is very little social role in the community; hence, it can be reasonably presumed that in Hinduism, individual faith is more crucial in reducing suicide. A study in Chennai found that the OR for lack of belief in God was 6.8 (CI 2.88–19.69) (Vijayakumar 2003). Those who committed suicide had less of a belief in God, changed their religious affiliation, and rarely visited the place of worship. A total of 11% had lost their faith in the three months prior to suicide. Gururaj et al. also found that lack of religious belief was a risk factor (OR 19.18; CI 4.17–10.37) (Gururaj et al. 2004).

There are numerous studies on attempted suicide in Asia. Unfortunately, different classifications, diagnostic systems, populations, and settings in the studies on attempted suicides defy any attempt to develop a common set of risk and protective factors.

Legal Issues

In India, attempted suicide is a punishable offense. Section 309 of the Indian Penal Code states that "whoever attempts to commit suicide and does any act towards the commission of such an offense shall be punished with simple imprisonment for a term which may extend to one year or with a fine or with both."

If the purpose of the law is to prevent suicide by legal methods, it is counter productive. Emergency care to those who have attempted suicide is denied, as many hospitals and practitioners hesitate to provide the needed treatment for of legal hassles. The actual data on attempted suicides becomes difficult to ascertain, as many attempts are assigned as accidental to avoid entanglement with police and courts.

Non Government Organizations (NGOs)

The mental health services are inadequate for the needs of the country. For a population of over one billion, there are only about 3,500 psychiatrists. Rapid urbanization, industrialization, and emerging family systems are resulting in social upheaval and distress. The diminishing traditional support systems leave people vulnerable. Hence, there is an emerging need for external emotional support. The enormity of the problem combined with the paucity of mental health services has led to the emergence of nongovernmental organizations (NGOs) in the field of suicide prevention.

Sneha was found in 1986 and, since its inception, has received 150,000 calls from the distressed. Sneha has actively supported, trained, and helped start centers at Hyderabad, New Delhi, Pondicherry, Thrissur, Cochin, Kolkatta, Ahmedabad, and Mumbai. All of them have come together to form Befrienders India. The primary aim of these centers is to provide emotional support to suicidal individuals through befriending. Often these centers function as an entry point for those needing professional services.

Nested Suicide Prevention Program

The concept of nested suicide prevention programs evolved when successful, relevant programs were identified, and the components of the suicide prevention measures were incorporated together.

Reducing the availability of the means to commit suicide is an important suicide prevention strategy. The majority of suicides in India are committed by poisoning, mainly by ingestion of organophosphorous compounds (pesticides). Forming an alliance with an environment activist group, the use of bio-fertilizers was promoted. A study to assess the relationship between suicide rates and consumption of pesticides in India was conducted.

A theater group was approached to perform street plays in the various tenements of the city of Chennai. These urban slums can best be described as overcrowded, unhygienic tenements and most of whose inhabitants are illiterate and work for daily wages. Street plays have had a long tradition in India. They are usually performed after 7 p.m. in an open place or street corner. The street plays focused on the themes of emotional distress, suicidal thoughts, the need to seek help, and possible support systems. The impact of the street plays was assessed by subsequent visits to these settlements. .

There are certain limitations in the activities of the NGOs. There is wide variability in the expertise of their volunteers and the services they provide. Quality control measures are inadequate, and most endeavors are not evaluated (Vijayakumar 2005b).

India grapples with infectious diseases, malnutrition, infant and maternal mortality, and other major health problems, even in this decade; hence, suicide is accorded low priority in the competition for meager resources.

There is an urgent need to develop a national plan for suicide prevention in India. The priority areas are: reducing the availability of and access to pesticide; reducing alcohol availability and consumption; promoting responsible media reporting of suicide and related issues: promoting and supporting NGOs; improving the capacity of primary care workers and specialist mental health services; providing support to those bereaved by suicide; and training the gatekeepers, such as teachers, police officers, practitioners of alternate systems of medicine, and faith healers.

Suicide is a multidimensional problem and, hence, suicide prevention programs should also be multidimensional. Collaboration, coordination, cooperation, and commitment are needed to develop and implement a national plan that is cost effective, appropriate, and relevant to the needs of the community.

In India, suicide prevention is more a social and public health objective than a traditional exercise in the mental health sector.

10

Conclusion and Reflections

Paul S.F. Yip

Suicide has become a worldwide public health concern. The situation is more serious in Asia in terms of the disability-adjusted life years (DALY) (*WHO* 2002). It is estimated that about 2.5% of loss of DALY is due to suicide and deliberate self-harm, and it is highest among different regions. We have selected eight countries/societies in the Asian region for our monograph, which, in total, cover nearly 50% of the world's population and more than 50% of suicides. For example, in China, the most highly populated country, it is estimated that more than 250,000 people commit suicide every year. Evidence suggests that men and women in rural areas are an important target group on which to focus in reducing the number of suicides in China (Yip et al. 2005a, 2008). A reduction in the number of suicides among men and women living in rural areas in China would have a significant worldwide impact. It is important that the cultural factors are better understood in order to formulate an effective suicide prevention program. For example, the pressure imposed on women relating to the one-child policy, a woman's status in China, and educational and employment opportunities are all important factors that could affect mental well-being. In addition, it is important to consider the power that the mass media has and its penetration into the community especially in Asian countries. The coverage of suicide news is always very explicit, graphical and sensational. A classic example is how information about poisoning by charcoal burning and its lethal effect spread throughout Hong Kong, the southern part of Guangzhou, Taiwan, and Japan. The leading cause of suicide in Taipei City in 2006 was charcoal burning; this was unheard of before the first case found in Hong Kong in 1997 (Liu et al., 2007; Yip and Lee, 2007).

It is gratifying that the Chinese government has become more receptive to recognizing the suicide problem. Limiting access to pesticides, especially in rural areas, and improving opportunities for education and quality of life (especially for women living in rural areas) seems to have led to a promising reduction in rates of suicide in China. However, suicide rates within urban regions (e.g., Beijing and Shanghai) are lower than in city-states, such as Hong Kong and Singapore. Therefore, it is logical to deduce that improved living conditions and improved medical and health care within rural regions can induce a sense of hope among people; this would be conducive for countries with the highest rates of suicide.

India, the second most populated country after China, has also experienced increasing rates of suicide, especially among women and young people. A high suicide rate in females may be related to a high prevalence of women suffering from marriage problems, including conflicts with in-laws. Religion is very much alive and part of Indian culture, and it is advantageous if religion provides spiritual support to the people. We understand that changing a deep-rooted and colorful culture is not an easy task. Apparently, suicide rates would be reduced if the external environment can be changed, that is, eliminating arranged marriages and exam stress especially among the young people. If the suicide rates within these two countries can be reduced, it would have an important impact on the global disease burden of suicide. It is estimated that the suicide rate could be reduced by at least 20% if the number of suicides in China and India were reduced by only 10%, due to the effect of their large populations .

Japan and South Korea share very similar suicide patterns and have had high suicide rates since the Asian financial turmoil in 1997. Recently, both countries have launched a national strategy for suicide prevention. Long working hours and a culture of not seeking help (especially among men) are some of the major barriers to suicide prevention. Furthermore, the two countries are experiencing a rapid transition in the labor market; the life-long job arrangement has changed, and some people have experienced problems adjusting to this change. Enhancing the working environment and identifying those at risk within the workplace could be effective in reducing suicide rates of middle-age men in both countries. It is particularly relevant when work- related suicide in Japan is serious. Furthermore, a recent study (Chan et al. 2007) showed that enhancing mental health through awareness programs, teaching problem-solving skills, and making available vocational training and job opportunities will provide much needed help for the unemployed.

Thailand, a very religious country (Buddhism), has experienced a recent increase in the suicide rate. Although the rate is still low in comparison to that of some other countries, the increasing trend is worrying. Buddhism is a religion that condemns suicide; however, the religion has somehow been misunderstood by some believers who think that they will enjoy a second life after committing suicide. In fact, according to Buddhist teachings, an individual will be worse off than they are presently if they commit suicide. It is a kind of untimely death which would not be rewarded. Additionally, the poverty and the spread of HIV/AIDS within the central regions of Thailand and the high suicide rates among HIV and AIDS patients are also worrying. Economically, economically deprived areas and high-risk groups should be areas of priority in the suicide prevention strategy in Thailand.

Taiwan has reached a historical high suicide rate that has increased by nearly 300% in the past ten years and shows no sign of slowing down. With a stagnant economy and unstable political conditions, suicide prevention may become even more difficult. There is a fear of job loss due to the poor economic conditions, and some manufacturing industries have been relocated to mainland China. Taiwan has also been seriously affected by the use of charcoal burning, which has become the leading cause of suicide in Taiwan; additionally, jumping to death from tall buildings in urban regions should be monitored carefully. Given such a high suicide rate and its rapid increasing trend, it is imperative that the Taiwan region need to address this issue with a matter of urgency. The method of charcoal burning poisoning death is of priority in restriction its accessibility.

In Singapore and Hong Kong, jumping from a high place is the leading method of suicide. The change of sovereignty in Hong Kong has not been shown to be directly linked to an increase in rates of suicide, although effective governance and an improving economic environment will definitely help make suicide prevention work easier. However, there are some serious problems currently facing Hong Kong. Marriage has been shown to be a protective factor, but fewer people are getting married. Within both countries, the increase in the proportion of people who have never married and divorced have had an adverse effect on suicide prevention effort. It is estimated more than 20% of the population would remain unmarried in the lifetime and the rate of divorce has increased ten times over the past two decades. The increase in divorce and domestic violence, and the disintegration of family support make it more difficult to utilize family resources to reduce the suicide rate in Hong Kong and other Asian cites that are experiencing similar problems.

Common Challenges

There are some common challenges for the countries included in this monograph, namely an incomplete or inaccurate monitoring and surveillance system for suicide death, especially in those countries that do not have a reliable and complete death registration system (e.g., India, China). It makes any evaluation program difficult, if not impossible, if we cannot establish accurate, baseline, suicide information.

Also, an increase in suicide rates among teenagers; relatively high suicide rates among older adults for both men and women; and a high case-fatality rate among suicide attempters due to the lethal methods used in these countries (e.g., pesticides in China and India, jumping in Hong Kong and Singapore, and hanging in South Korea and Japan) pose real challenges for suicide prevention in Asia. All these methods are easily available and highly effective. Community support and participation in preventing suicides in Asia is not only desirable but essential if there is any chance to succeed. However, some of the programs that have been set up for suicide prevention are not conducted in an organized, integrated, or holistic manner. The commitment and resources from the governments of these countries is still relatively low compared to developed Western countries. Furthermore, resources for health and medical services are inadequate to provide the necessary psychological treatment and services for depressed individuals. Additionally, stigmatization exists towards the mentally ill, and the help-seeking behavior among the needy is poor. At the same time, the estimated loss of labor productivity due to suicide is high; this is partly due to the increasing rate of suicide among the young and middle aged (Yip et al. 2005b, 2008).

A Public Health Approach to Suicide Prevention

The burden of suicide in Asian countries can no longer be ignored. Suicides have a significant impact on economic growth and development. Unfortunately, the majority of suicidal people are reluctant to seek help from health care professionals, probably because of many cultural factors: suicide is still seen as a taboo subject that is not widely discussed in the community; stigma towards treatment; limited availability of treatment; and uncertainty about treatment effectiveness. Suicide has traditionally been viewed as a mental health issue that is addressed primarily through clinical intervention, especially the treatment of depression. However, it has been suggested that the role of mental illness within suicide is not as significant as it is in the West (Phillips et al. 2002; Yip et al. 2005a, b). Also, it is known that approximately two-thirds of all people who commit suicide did not receive any specialist psychiatric care in the year before their death (CSRP 2005). The World Health Organization (WHO) and many national suicide prevention strategies (for example, those in the USA, Australia, Ireland, New Zealand, and the UK) have proposed a public health approach aimed at dealing with suicide prevention, rather than treating it as a medical problem only.

The public health approach involves three layers of intervention: universal, selective, and *indicative* (Table 1). This public health approach acknowledges the importance of both high-risk and population-based strategies of suicide prevention, and requires a multi-sector effort to tackle the problem at multiple levels: in the community (*universal* strategies), among specific population subgroups (*selective* strategies), and among those at a particularly high risk of suicidal behavior (*indicative* strategies).

Table 1. Universal, Selective, and Indicative Preventive Interventions.

Strategy	Definition	Examples
Universal	For everyone in a population	Public education programs about the dangers of substance abuse
Selective	For target subgroups at particular risk of suicide	Programs for the children of parents with manic depressive illness or victims of physical sexual abuse, unemployed
Indicative	For specific individuals who, at examination, have a risk factor or condition that puts them at a very high risk	Programs for people who already have had suicidal ideation or have made previous attempts

The public health approach is particularly apt for suicide prevention in Asian countries. Flooding is a common problem in Asia, and it can be used as a useful metaphor for suicide prevention. When a flood occurs, rescue teams work hard to save those affected, focusing attention mainly on the victims who are swept downstream. Indeed, this is very important, otherwise lives will be lost. However, in the long term, it is important that the causes of the flood (e.g., upstream conditions such as deforestation, over-cultivation, pollution, etc.) are ascertained in order to prevent further flooding. What lies "upstream" of the increasing number of suicides is often a malfunctioning and disconnected society. A disconnected community, the breakdown of the traditional family support system, and a stressful and uncaring community culture, unhealthy working practices are important correlates of suicidality in the respective communities.

By virtue of its systematic approach to prevent illness, disability, and premature death, the public health strategy provides a strong framework for creating an effective and concerted effort to prevent suicide. In other words, public health interventions not only tackle the "downstream" problems, but also aim to improve the "upstream" conditions. The Rose Theorem states that a large number of people exposed to a low risk may generate more cases than a small number of people who are exposed to a high risk (Rose 1992). The proverb "an ounce of prevention is better than an ounce of cure" echoes the idea behind this insight. Figure 1 further illustrates this philosophy: by reducing the suicidal risk of the population at large (shifting the distribution of the suicidal risk of the whole population to the left), fewer people will have a very high risk of suicide (reduction in the area under the "danger zone"). Hence, a partnership among mental health professionals and different sectors of the community should target the larger populations before any "symptoms" appear, and the risk of suicide becomes imminent.

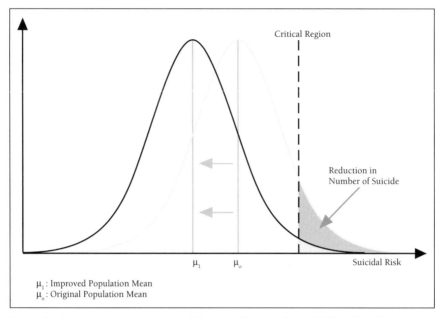

Figure 1   A schematic representation of the Rose Theorem (Rose 1992) and Yip (2005)

On the basis of rigorous calculations, Lewis et al. (1997) have shown that high-risk (indicative) strategies would only have a modest effect on suicide rates within a population, even if effective interventions were developed, and the UK government's target for suicide reduction was more likely to be achieved using population-based strategies that aimed at actively reducing risk among the whole population. Furthermore, research has shown that suicide can be the tragic endpoint of the interplay of a wide range of factors, including biological, genetic, social, cultural, psychological, and behavioral factors. For these reasons, it is imperative that multiple avenues and the three approaches of intervention should be considered together for suicide prevention and intervention. As the eminent psychiatrist Keith Hawton (Centre for Suicide Research, University of Oxford, UK) put it: "Suicide rates are unlikely to decline as long as we confine our prevention efforts only to those who are at immediate risk of attempting suicide." (Yip 2005)

The Hong Kong Experience: Some Initiatives and Reflections

Hong Kong has demonstrated some unique examples of suicide prevention that would be of interest and relevance to other countries. We strongly believe that one size does not fit all. The differences in the strategies being adopted in different countries are related to the different stages of economic development that countries have reached. The importance of the availability of resources for suicide prevention cannot be understated. There is always cost involved for any suicide prevention effort, but the potential benefit for preventing suicide will outweigh its cost. There are some important ingredients from suicide prevention strategies in Hong Kong that can be applied to other countries. One example is government commitment: it is important to have support from the government to do any suicide prevention work in the community. Raising awareness of the importance of mental health can be more cost-effective if the government is willing to come on board and provide help. Support from the government cannot be taken for granted. In some situations, mental health and suicide prevention is not high on their list of priorities and will not be given the requested support. However, schools and other government departments and agencies can be effective mediums through which to communicate the message across the community. The Hong Kong Jockey Club Centre for Suicide Research and Prevention (CSRP) at The University of Hong Kong was established in 2002 and is supported by the Chief Executive Community Fund that provides resources for projects which can provide direct benefit to the community. The centre was set up during a time of increased suicide rates in the community, and the government was under pressure to do something. An international advisory committee that consisted of esteemed suicide research scholars was set up and is chaired by the Secretary of Justice (Ms Elsie Leung, a senior government official) at the time.

We have also managed to build channels to communicate our opinion that mass media reporting on suicide is an issue of great importance. The rapid spread of suicide by poisoning through charcoal burning is very much related to the sensational and overwhelmingly detailed description of the method to the community (Liu et al. 2006; Chan et al. 2005; Yip et al. 2006).

The nongovernmental organizations (NGOs) that are working on suicide prevention in Hong Kong have formed an alliance so that each stakeholder can be better informed about the latest knowledge and developments. Despite some differences in expectations and logistics among suicide prevention agencies, communication in the community has been improved and expanded. The CSRP has also actively participated in providing training to frontline individuals, such as teachers, social workers, and insurance agents. The CSRP's website on depression, entitled "Little Prince is Depressed" (www.depression.edu.hk), has won the Silver Innovation award (*Asian Wall Street Journal*) and the Hong Kong-based best ten meritorious awards for its innovation and creativity in reaching out to the public and destigmatizing depression. This effort can be seen as part of the universal intervention program for the community.

A community project for suicide prevention has been launched by the Hong Kong Police Force in one of the districts on Hong Kong Island. The stakeholders in the community, including many Government departments, for example, housing department, social work department, schools, district office, police, and hospitals, are part of the community task force. One of the objectives is to raise awareness of the problem of suicide in the community, thereby improving the connectedness among stakeholders who seek to further improve the care provided for suicide-attempt survivors. The project is inspired by a successful community-based suicide prevention effort on Cheung Chau Island, which is a popular getaway destination in Hong Kong. After a local visitor committed suicide by burning charcoal in a holiday flat in 1998, the island became a notoriously popular place to commit suicide. To tackle the problem, local representatives of the island initiated a joint effort to prevent further suicides; this involved a partnership among community members, the police, and mental health care professionals. In the two years since the program was implemented, suicide rates have decreased substantially. This example illustrates the effectiveness of a timely in-person crisis intervention and community-based gate keeping in preventing suicide, and has strengthened the belief that suicide is preventable. Prevention needs the involvement of the whole community, including volunteers. Implementing a neighborhood watch scheme and strengthening the community network seem to be promising measures that can prevent suicide at the community level (Wong et al. 2008; Knox et al. 2003).

Other community-based suicide prevention efforts have been implemented in the last few years: the CARElink service in the police department and Greenpasture in the public hospital system, which are tailored to provide counseling and support services to the police force, and medical and health workers, respectively.

Regarding selective intervention, there is a special program for pathological gamblers and mental illness. Additional efforts and resources from the government have been channeled to those districts where higher suicide rates are found. Consideration is also being given to youth mentoring programs for young people with suicidal risk in the community (e.g. Peter Lee's Youth Mentoring Program). Training is also provided for medical doctors and allied health care workers in order to raise their awareness and enhance their competence to deal with suicidal patients.

Regarding indicative strategies, which are especially helpful for those who have deliberately self-harmed, efforts have been made in accident and emergency (A&E) departments to enhance the treatment protocol and discharge plan because a significant proportion of suicide reattempts are admitted to A&E departments. It has been shown that making use of existing community resources to enhance drug compliance, family acceptance, and employment opportunities is crucial for reducing suicidality among people with mental illness (Yim et al. 2004). The police have implemented training programs so that frontline staff are better able to deal with deliberate self-harm and domestic violence calls.

Our psychological autopsy study (Chen et al. 2006) and prevalence study (Liu et al. 2006) suggest that the important risk factors are psychiatric problems; unemployment; unmanageable debts; poor social problem-solving skills; and being separated, divorced, widowed, or never married. Depression is an important risk factor for suicidal behavior. However, having good coping skills, a strong family, and a strong social support system, and being socially connected and responsible to one's family make people more resilient to adverse life situations. These findings suggest that if suicide prevention efforts only make use of medical and health care professionals, the effect on suicide reduction would be limited. Suicide prevention efforts need to tackle multiple causes of suicide and suicidal behavior by addressing all possible avenues. Such efforts may include enhancing mental health education, empowering families to function better, improving the community network, and, more specifically, restricting access to the means of committing suicide.

The need for an effective suicide prevention program in Hong Kong is clear. However, one of the most challenging concerns in offering a suicide prevention program is the lack of objective evidence on the effectiveness of such a program. Policymakers and stakeholders often do not have adequate information on what makes an effective prevention program. Evaluation is very important, and it is essential for directing the use of scarce resources as well as for constantly improving services. Therefore, there is an urgent need to develop local skills through rigorous evaluation. It is also important to make evaluation a necessary, rather than auxiliary or optional, component of local prevention efforts. A measure of the effectiveness of suicide prevention efforts is the reduction in the level of suicidal behavior in the community.

We are appealing to the governments in this region to develop a universal approach that prioritizes suicide as one of the leading problems in the community which need to be addressed. This includes providing funding and logistical support for suicide research and prevention. Additionally, the mass media plays an influential part in suicide prevention. It is a two-edged sword that, if not managed correctly, will make vulnerable people follow suit by romanticizing suicide as a way to resolve problems. International efforts are being made by the WHO and other organizations that are trying to work in partnership with the media to get them to participate in suicide prevention work.

People are sometimes skeptical of the effectiveness of restricting access to the means of committing suicide; however, research does suggest that this is an evidence-based suicide prevention effort (Liu et al. 2007). By restricting such access, we are buying time, which allows more opportunities for intervention.

Regarding the selective approach, there are certain groups who are at high risk of suicide: women living in rural China, the unemployed, those who suffer from mental illness, and those experiencing family violence and divorce. It might be worthwhile to consider certain programs, and some tailor-made programs might be more effective in helping those in high-risk groups. For a selective program to work, it might be necessary to procure additional resources to do the work properly; however, it is important to be able to make use of community resources. For example, with community support, this relatively high-risk group (e.g., ex-mental health patients) can be reintegrated into the community more successfully which has been shown to be significant in reducing the suicide risk among the ex-mental health patients. (Yim et al. 2004)

Regarding indicative intervention, which is especially helpful for those who have made previous suicide attempts, it is important that the management of existing health care systems be improved for these groups. Suicide risk among recently discharged mental health patients is particularly high, and the treatment protocol for those who have deliberately self-harmed and have been admitted to hospital needs to be carefully monitored. Research also shows that for people who have made a previous suicide attempt, their suicidal risk increases by 60%–300%; therefore, we need to try and understand their needs better so that more effective services can be provided to them.

National Suicide Prevention Strategy: Are We Ready?

National Suicide Prevention Strategy has been launched by many different countries: the USA, England, Scotland, Australia, New Zealand, Finland, and Norway. They have developed comprehensive national suicide prevention strategies that incorporate a public health approach. National strategies for suicide prevention in these countries share a number of common elements, including the use of educational settings as sites of intervention; attempts to change the portrayal of suicidal behavior and mental illness in the media; efforts to increase and improve the detection and treatment of depression and other mental illness; an emphasis on reducing the stigma associated with help-seeking behaviors; strategies designed to improve access to services; promotion of effective preventive efforts with rigorous evaluation; and efforts to reduce access to the means of suicide. In learning from other countries, Hong Kong should place great value on implementing a similar public health approach; however, the Hong Kong government has yet to endorse a national strategy campaign.

Indeed, suicide is everyone's business. Not all suicides are preventable, but we certainly can make a difference. The suicide problem in Asia is huge. The cost is high. Every year, more than 500,000 people die from suicide in this part of the world. Increased research and prevention in this region will not only reduce the suicide rate in Asia, but the information and evidence will be of benefit to the West as well. Despite limited resources, we can make a contribution. Suicide is not only a problem in Asia and the stakes are high, so let us spare no effort in combating the rise of this tragedy.

References

Preface

World Health Organization (2002). World report on violence and health. Geneva: WHO.

CHAPTER 2 (JAPAN)

Chiu, H. F. K., Takahashi, Y., and Suh, G. H. (2003). Elderly suicide prevention in Asia. *International Journal of Geriatric Psychiatry*, 18: 973–6.

Conner, K.R., Beautries A.L., and Conwell, Y. (2003) Risk factors for suicide and medically serious attempts among alcoholics: analyses of Centebury Suicide Project data. *Journal Study of Alcohol*, 64:551–554.

Durkheim, E. (1951). Suicide — A study in sociology. Trans.J. A. Spaulding and G. Simpson. London: Routledge and Kegan Paul Ltd.

Japan Medical Association (2004). *Suicide prevention manual for primary care physicians.* Tokyo: Akashi-shoten. (written in Japanese)

Miki, O. (2002). The clinical feature of depression with psychosomatic medicine in primary care. *Japanese Journal of Psychosomatic Medicine*, 42: 585–91.

National Police Agency (2004). *Summary document on the suicide incidents in 2003.* Tokyo: National Police Agency. (written in Japanese)

Takahashi, Y. (1992). *Suicide risk: clinical evaluation and suicide intervention.* Tokyo: Kongo-shuppan. (written in Japanese)

Takahashi, Y. (1998). *Suicidal sings.* Tokyo: Kongo-shuppan. (written in Japanese)

Takahashi, Y. (2003). *Suicide in the middle age.* Tokyo: Kodansha. (written in Japanese)

Takahashi K., Naito H., Morita M., et al. (1998). Suicide prevention for the elderly in Matsunoyama Town, Higashikubiki County, Niigata Prefecture: psychiatric care for elderly depression in the community. *Seishin Shinkeigaku Zasshi*, 100: 469–85. (written in Japanese)

World Health Organization (2003). *Suicide rate.* WHO Home Page http://www.who.int/mental_health/prevention/suicide/suiciderates/en/ Geneva: WHO.

Chapter 3 (South Korea)

Chandler, M. J., Lalonde, C. E., Sokol, B. W., and Hallett, D. (2003). *Personal persistence, identity development, and suicide: A study of native and non-native North American adolescents.* Monograph of the Society for Research in Child Development, ed. Willis F. Overton. Boston: Blackwell Publishing.

Chuang, H. L. and Huang, W. C. (1996). A re-examination of "sociological and economic theories of suicide: A comparison of the U.S.A. and Taiwan." *Social Science and Medicine,* 43: 421–3.

Clayer, J. R. and Czechowicz, A. S. (1991). Suicide by Aboriginal people in South Australia: Comparison with suicide deaths in the total urban and rural populations. *Medical Journal of Australia,* 154: 683–5.

Doan, T. (1990). *Regression analysis of time series.* Evanston, IL: Var Econometrics.

Durkheim, E. (1951). *Suicide : A Study in Sociology.* New York: Free Press. (Originally published in 1897)

Johnson, B. D. (1965). Durkheim's one cause of suicide. *American Sociological Review,* 30: 875–86.

Lester, D. (1994). Suicide and unemployment: A monthly analysis. *Psychological Reports,* 75: 602.

Lester, D. (1995). American Indian suicide rates and the economy. *Psychological Reports,* 77: 994.

Lester, D., and Yang, B. (1998). *Suicide and homicide in the twentieth century.* Commack, NY: Nova Science.

Lester, D. and Yang B. (2003). Unemployment and suicidal behaviour. *Journal of Epidemiology and Community Health,* 57: 558–9.

Mannheim, K. (1952). *Essays on the sociology of knowledge.* London: Routledge and Kegan Paul.

Park, J. S., Lee, J. Y., and Kim, S. D. (2003). A study for effects of economic growth rate and unemployment rate to suicide rate in Korea. *Korean Journal of Preventive Medicine,* 36: 85–91.

Yip, P. S. F. (1996). Suicide in Hong Kong, Taiwan and Beijing, *British Journal of Psychiatry,* 169: 495–500.

Yip, P. S. F. and Tan, R. C. E. (1998). Suicide in Hong Kong and Singapore: A tale of two cities. *International Journal of Social Psychiatry,* 44: 267–79.

Chapter 4 (Mainland China)

Banister, J. and Preston, S. H. (1981). Mortality in China. *Population and Development Review,* 7: 98–110.

Cheng, A. T. (1995). Mental illness and suicide. A case-control study in east Taiwan. *Archives of General Psychiatry,* 52: 594–603.

Durkheim, E. (1897[1951]) *Suicide: A study in sociology,* trans. G. Simpson. London: Routledge and Kegan Paul.

Knox, K. L., Litts, D. A., Talcott, G. W., et al. (2003). Risk of suicide and related adverse outcomes after exposure to a suicide prevention in the U.S. Air Force: Cohort study. *British Medical Journal,* 327: 1376–80.

Murray, C. J. L. and Lopez, A. D. (1996). *Global health statistics*. Cambridge: Harvard University Press.

Pearson, V. and Liu, M. (2002). Ling's death: An ethnography of a Chinese woman's suicide. *Suicide and Life-Threatening Behavior*, 32: 347–58.

Pearson, V., Phillips, M. R., He, F., et al. (2002) Attempted suicide among young rural women in the People's Republic of China: Possibilities for prevention. *Suicide and Life-Threatening Behavior*, 32: 359–69.

Phillips, M. R., Li, X., and Zhang, Y. (2002). Suicide rates in China, 1995–99. *Lancet*, 359: 835–40.

Phillips, M. R., Liu, H., and Zhang, Y. (1999). Suicide and social change in China. *Culture Medicine and Psychiatry*, 23: 25–50.

Phillips, M. R., Yang, G., Zhang, Y., et al. (2002). Risk factors for suicide in China: A national case-control psychological autopsy study. *Lancet*, 360: 1728–36.

World Health Organization (1998). Guidelines for the primary prevention of mental, neurological and psychosocial disorders. Geneva: WHO .

World Health Organization (2003). *Suicide rate*. WHO Home Page http://www.who.int/ mental_health/prevention/suicide/suiciderates/en/ Geneva: WHO.

Yip, P. S. F. (1998). Age, sex, marital status and suicide: An empirical study of East and West. *Psychological Reports*, 82: 311–22.

Yip, P. S. F., Liu, K. Y., Hu, J., Song, X.M. (2005). Suicide rates in China during a decade of rapid social changes. *Social Psychiatry and Psychiatric Epidemiology*, 40: 792–8.

Yip, P. S. F. and Thorburn, J. (2004). Marital status and the risk of suicide: experience from England and Wales, 1982–1996. *Psychological Reports*, 94: 401–7.

Yip, P. S. F., Callanan, C., and Yuen, H. P. (2000). Urban/rural and gender differentials in suicide rates: East and west. *Journal of Affective Disorders*, 57: 99–106.

Yip, P. S. F. and Liu, K. Y. (2006). The Ecological Fallacy and the Gender Ratio in China. *British Journal of Psychiatry*, 189: 465–466.

Chapter 5 (Hong Kong)

Centre for Suicide Research and Prevention (2005). *Research findings into suicide and its prevention*. The Hong Kong Jockey Club Centre for Suicide Research and Prevention, The University of Hong Kong.

Census and Statistics Department.(1990–2004) *Registered Death in Hong Kong*. HKSAR.

Census and Statistics Department. (2004). *Hong Kong population projections 2004–2033*. HKSAR.

Chan, K. P. M., Lee, D. T. S., and Yip, P. S. F. (2003). Media influence on suicide. Media's role is double edged. *British Medical Journal*, 326(7387): 498.

Chan, K. P. M., Yip, P. S. F, Au, J., and Lee, D. T. S. (2005). Charcoal burning suicide in post-transition Hong Kong. *British Journal of Psychiatry*, 186: 67–71.

Chan, S. M., Chiu, F. K., Lam, C. W., et al. (2006). Elderly suicide and the 2003 SARS epidemic in Hong Kong. *International Journal of Geriatric Psychiatry*, 21(2): 113–8.

Coroner's Court (2005). *Coroner's Report 2005*. Judiciary, Hong Kong.

International Labour Office. (1990). *International standard classification of occupations: ISCO-88*. Geneva.

Lee, D. T. S, Chan, K. P. M, Lee, S., and Yip, P. S. F. (2002). Burning charcoal: A novel and contagious method of suicide in Asia. *Archives of General Psychiatry*, 59: 293–4.

Liu, K. Y., Beautrais, A., Caine, E., Chan, K., Chao, A., Conwell, Y., Law C, Lee D, Li P, Yip R. S. F. (2007) Charcoal burning suicides in Hong Kong and urban Taiwan: an illustration of the impact of a novel suicide method on overall regional rates. *Journal of Epidemiology and Community Health*, 61(3), 248–253.

Lo, W. H. and Leung, T. M. (1985). Suicide in Hong Kong. *Australian and New Zealand Journal of Psychiatry*, 19: 287–92.

Murray, C. J. L. (1996). Rethinking DALYs. In *The global burden of disease*, ed. C. J. L. Murray and A. D. Lopez. 1–98.Cambridge: Harvard University Press.

Takahashi, Y. (2004). Improving portrayal of suicide reporting in the media. National Strategies for Suicide Prevention: An International Workshop, Aug 15–20, Salzburg.

World Bank Group. (2004). World Development Indicators 2004. http://www.worldbank.org/data/wdi2004. Assessed on 13 October 2004.

World Health Organization. (1978). *The ninth revision of the International Classification of Diseases and related health problems* (9th ed.) (ICD-9). Geneva: WHO.

World Health Organization. (1992). *The tenth revision of the International Classification of Diseases and related health problems* (10th ed.) (ICD-10). Geneva: WHO.

World Health Organization. (2002). *World Health Report 2002*. Geneva.

Yip, P. S. F. (1996). Suicides in Hong Kong, Taiwan and Beijing 1981–1994. *British Journal of Psychiatry*, 169: 495–500.

Yip, P. S. F. (1997). Suicide in Hong Kong 1981–1994. *Social Psychiatry and Psychiatric Epidemiology*, 32: 243–50.

Yip, P. S. F. and Chi, I. (2001). *Suicide behaviour in Hong Kong elderly. Suicide and euthanasia in older adults: A transcultural journey*, ed. Diego DeLeo. 97–115. *Göttingen*, Germany: Hogrefe and Huber Publishers.

Yip, P. S. F., Law C. K. and Law, F. Y. W. (2003). Suicide in Hong Kong: Epidemiological profile and burden analysis. *Hong Kong Medical Journal*, 9: 419–426.

Yip, P. S. F and Lee, D. T. S. (2007) Charcoal Burning suicides and strategies for prevention *Journal of Crisis Intervention and Suicide Prevention*, 28 (suppl. 1) 21–27.

Chapter 6 (Taiwan)

Chan, K. P., Yip, P. S., Au, J., and Lee, D. T. (2005). Charcoal burning suicide in post-transition Hong Kong. *British Journal of Psychiatry*, 186: 67–73.

Cheng, A. T. A. (1995). Mental illness and suicide: A case-control study in East Taiwan. *Archives of General Psychiatry*, 52: 594–603.

Cheng, A. T. A., Chen, T. H. H., Chen, C. C., and Jenkins, R. (2000). Psychosocial and psychiatric risk factors for suicide: Case-control psychological autopsy study. *British Journal of Psychiatry*, 177: 360–5.

Cheng, A. T. A., Hawton, K., Lee, C. T. and Chen, T. H. (2007a) The influence of media reporting of the suicide of a celebrity on suicide rates: a population-based study. *International Journal of Epidemiology*, 36(6): 1229–34.

Cheng, A. T. A., Hawton, K., Chen, T. H., Yen, A. M., Chen, C. Y., Chen, L. C. and Teng, P. R. (2007b) The influence of media coverage of a celebrity suicide on subsequent suicide attempts. *Journal of Clinical Psychiatry*, 68(6):862–4.

Chong, M. and Cheng, T. A. (1995). Suicidal behaviour observed in Taiwan: Trends over four decades. In *Chinese society and mental health*, ed. T. Y. Lin, W. S. Tseng, and H. K. Yeh. 209–18. Oxford University Press.

Chou, Y. J., Huang, N., Lee, C. H., et al. (2003). Suicides after the 1999 Taiwan earthquake. *International Journal of Epidemiology*, 32: 1007–14.

Department of Health (DOH) (1983–2006) Health and National Health Insurance Annual Statistics Information Service. ERLINK "http://www.doh.gov.tw/statistic/" http://www.doh.gov.tw/statistic/, Department of Health, Executive Yuan, Taiwan.

Department of Household Registration Affairs (2006). *Population by age in Taiwan-Fuchien Area 1974–2005*. Taiwan: Ministry of Interior.

Government Information Office (GIO) (2007). Taiwan Yearbook 2006. http://www.gio.gov.tw/taiwan-website/5-gp/yearbook/contents.html. Accessed on 22 December 2007.

Lloyd, C. J. and Yip, P. S. F. (2001). A comparison of suicide patterns in Australia and Hong Kong. *Journal of Royal Statistical Society*, 164: 467–83.

Taiwan Agricultural Chemicals and Toxic Substances Research Institute (TACTRI) (2007). The official website of Taiwan Agricultural Chemicals and Toxic Substances Research Institute. http://www.tactri.gov.tw. Accessed on 22 December 2007.

Taiwan Headlines (2007) ww.taiwanheadlines.gov.tw/" http://www.taiwanheadlines.gov.tw/ Accessed on 29 December 2007.

Taiwan Suicide Prevention Center (TSPC) (2007). The official website of Taiwan Suicide Prevention Center. http://www.tspc.doh.gov.tw/index.html. Accessed on 22 December 2007.

Tzeng, G. H. and Wu, T. Y. (1986). Characteristics of urbanization levels in Taiwan districts. *Geographical Research*, 12: 287–323.

World Health Organization (1978). *The ninth revision of the International Classification of Diseases and related health problems* (9th ed.) (ICD-9). Geneva: WHO.

World Health Organization (1999). *Injury: a leading cause of the global burden of disease*. Geneva: WHO.

World Health Organization (2001). *World Health Report 2001*. Geneva: WHO.

World Health Organization (2005). Meeting on suicide prevention in the western Pacific region. Manila, The Philippines.

Yip, P. S. F. (1996). Suicide in Hong Kong, Taiwan and Beijing. *British Journal of Psychiatry*, 169: 495–500.

Yip, P. S. F., Law, C. K., and Law, Y. W. (2003). Suicide in Hong Kong: Epidemiological profile and burden analysis, 1981–2001. *Hong Kong Medical Journal*, 9: 419–26.

Yip, P. S. F. and Lee, D. T. S. (2007) Charcoal burning suicides and strategies for prevention. *Journal of Crisis Intervention and Suicide Prevention*, 28 (suppl. 1): 21-27.

Yip, P. S. F. and Thorburn, J. (2004). Marital status and the risk of suicide: Experience from England and Wales, 1982–1996. *Psychological Reports*, 94: 401–7.

Chapter 7 (Thailand)

Aufderheide, T. P., Aprahamian, C., Mateer, J. R., et al. (1994). Emergency airway management in hanging victims. *Annals of Emergency Medicine*, 24: 879–84.

Beautrais, A. (2006). Suicide prevention strategies 2006. *Australian e-Journal for the Advancement of Mental Health*, 5 (1). (http://www.auseinet.com/journal/vol5iss1/beautraiseditorial.pdf).

Bertolote, J. M. and Fleischman, A. (2002). A global perspective on the epidemiology of suicide. *Suicidologi*, 7: 6–8.

Chartananondh, T., Mahatnirunkul, S., and Phumpaisalchai, W. (1999). Stress, coping style and suicidal idea among Thai people in the time of economic crises. *Journal of Mental Health of Thailand*, 7: 29–36. (in Thai)

Chayovan, N. and Knodel, J. (1997). *A report on the survey of the welfare of the elderly in Thailand*. Bangkok: Institute of Population Studies, Chulalongkorn University.

Choowattanapakorn, T. (1999). The social situation in Thailand: The impact on elderly people. *International Journal of Nursing Practice*, 5: 95–9.

Choprapawan, C. (2003). *A study of the cause of death of Thai people in 16 provinces who died between 1997 and 1999*. Bangkok: Ministry of Public Health. (in Thai)

Department of Diseases Control (2006). *A review of HIV/AIDS management and prevention during 2002–2006*. Bangkok: Department of Diseases Control, Ministry of Public Health. (http://www.aidsthai.org/download/total_report_group_misson.doc). (in Thai)

Department of Mental Health (2000). *Survey results of mental health condition of the people during the economic crisis, by telephone communication*. Bangkok: Department of Mental Health, Ministry of Public Health. (in Thai)

Eddleston, M., Karunaratne, A., Weerakoon, M., et al. (2006). Choice of poison for intentional self-poisoning in rural Sri Lanka. *Clinical Toxicology*, 44: 283–6.

Eddleston, M., Karalliedde, L., Buckley, N., et al. (2002). Pesticide poisoning in the developing world — a minimum pesticides list. *Lancet*, 360: 1163–7.

Fordham, G. (1995). Whisky, women and song: Men, alcohol and AIDS in northern Thailand — Thai sexuality in the age of AIDS. *The Australian Journal of Anthropology*, 6: 154–77.

Gray, R., Rakumnuaykit, P., and Kittisuksathit, S. (2006). Happiness based on self-sufficiency: Security in later life. In *Population and society 2006*, ed. K. Archavanichkul and V. Thongthai. 114–25. Nakorn Pathom: Institute of Population and Social Research. (in Thai)

Gunnell, D., Bennewith, O., Hawton, K., et al. (2005). The epidemiology and prevention of suicide by hanging: A systematic review. *International Journal of Epidemiology*, 34: 433–42.

Institute for Population and Social Research (2007). Population of Thailand 2007. *Mahidol Population Gazette*, 16.

Isarabhakdi, P. (1995). *Determinants of sexual behaviour that influence the risk of pregnancy and disease among rural Thai young adults*. Nakorn Pathom: Institute for Population and Social Research.

Kitayama, S. and Markus, H. (1994). *Emotion and culture*. Washington,D.C.: APA Press.

Knodel, J., Chayovan, N., Graiurapong, S. et al. (2000). Ageing in Thailand: An overview of formal and informal support. In *Ageing in the Asia-Pacific Regions: Issues and Policies*, ed. Phillips, D. 243–66. London: Routledge and Kegan Paul.

Kposowa, A. J. (2000). Marital status and suicide in the National Longitudinal Mortality Study. *Journal of Epidemiology and Community Health*, 54: 254–61.

Kreitman, N. (1988). Suicide, age and marital status. *Psychological Medicine*, 18: 121–8.

Lindesay, J. (1986). Trends in self-poisoning in the elderly 1974–1983. *International Journal of Psychogeriatric Psychiatry*, 1: 37–43.

Lotrakul, M. (2005). Suicide in the North of Thailand. *Journal of the Medical Association of Thailand*, 88: 944–8.

Lotrakul, M., Thanapaisal, A., and Gegina, S. (2000). *Lived experience of males and females who attemped suicide*. Bangkok: Duangkamol. (in Thai)

Mann, J. J., Apter, A., Bertolote, J., et al. (2005). Suicide prevention strategies: A systematic review. *Journal of the American Medical Association*, 294: 2064–74.

Marzuk, P. M., Leon, A. C., Tardiff, K., et al. (1992). The effect of access to lethal methods of injury on suicide rates. *Archive of General Psychiatry*, 49: 451–8.

Mongkol, A. (2003). Epidemiology of attempted suicide and complete suicide. Proceedings of the Second International Conference on Mental Health and Substance Dependence, Aug 19–21,2003, Bangkok, Thailand. (in Thai)

Mongkol, A., Tangseri, T., Pimsen, S., et al. (2005). *A study report of completed suicide*. Bangkok: Department of Mental Health. (in Thai)

Moodie, R., Borthwick, C., Phongphit1, S., et al. (2000). Health promotion in South-East Asia: Indonesia, DPR Korea, Thailand, the Maldives and Myanmar. *Health Promotion International*, 15: 249–57.

Narongchai, P. (1995). Suicidal cases in Maharaj Nakorn Chiangmai hospital. *Chiangmai Medical Bulletin*, 34: 15–21. (in Thai)

Neeleman, J., Wessely, S., and Lewis, G. (1998). Suicide acceptability in African and White Americans: the role of religion. *Journal of Nervous and Mental Disease*, 186: 12–6.

Phillips, M. R., Yang, H. G., Zhang, Y., et al. (2002). Risk factors for suicide in China: A national case-control psychological autopsy study. *Lancet*, 360: 1728–36.

Phillips, M. R., Liu, H., and Zhang, Y. (1999). Suicide and social change in China. *Culture, Medicine and Psychiatry*, 23: 25–50.

Pritchard, C. (1996). Suicide in the People's Republic of China categorized by age and gender: Evidence of the influence of culture on suicide. *Acta Psychiatrica Scandinavica*, 93: 362–7.

Qin, P., Agerbo, E., and Mortensen, P. B. (2003). Suicide risk in relation to socioeconomic, demographic, psychiatric, and familial factors: A national register-based study of all suicides in Denmark, 1981–1997. *American Journal of Psychiatry*, 160: 765–72.

Ratanakul, P. (2004). The Buddhist concept of life, suffering and death, and related bioethical issues. *Eubios Journal of Asian and International Bioethics*, 14: 141–6.

Siriboon, S. (1993). *Facts and attitudes among Thai adults toward caring of the elderly*. Bangkok: Research Division Chulalongkorn University. (in Thai)

Sobieszczyk, T., Knodel, J., and Napaporn, C. (2003). Gender and Well-Being Among the Elderly: Evidence From Thailand. *Ageing & Society*, 23: 701-35..

Somboontanont, T., Visrutratana, S., Tantipiwatanaskul, P., et al. (2000). Suicide: Comparison factors and characteristics of victims related to suicide before and during the economic crisis. *Journal of Mental Health of Thailand*, 8: 1–7. (in Thai)

Takahashi, Y., Hirasawa, H., Koyama, K., et al. (1998). Suicide in Japan: Present state and future directions for prevention. *Transcultural Psychiatry*, 35: 271–89.

Tangcharoensathien, V., Faramnuayphol, P., Teokul, W., et al. (2006). A critical assessment of mortality statistics in Thailand: Potential for improvements. *Bulletin of the World Health Organization*, 84: 233–8.

Tantipiwatanaskul, P. and Visrutratana, S. (1998). *Suicide: An investigation and prevention.* Bangkok: Department of Mental Health. (in Thai)

Thapinta, A. and Hudak, P. F. (2000). Pesticide use and residual occurrence in Thailand. *Environmental Monitoring and Assessment,* 60: 103–14.

United Nations Development Programme (2004). *Thailand's response to HIV/AIDS: Progress and challenges.* Bangkok: UNDP.

Vijayakumar, L. (2008). Suicide and suicide prevention in India. In Suicide and Suicide Prevention in Asia edited Paul S.F. Yip. The Hong Kong University Press.

Vijayakumar, L., John, S., Pirkis, J., et al. (2005). Suicide in developing countries (2): Risk factors. *Crisis,* 26: 112–9.

Wibulpolprasert, S., Gajeena, A., Ekachampaka, P. et al. (2002). *Thailand Health Profile 1999–2000.* Bangkok: Bureau of Policy and Strategy, Ministry of Public Health.

World Bank (2001). *Thailand Economic Monitor 2001.* Bangkok: World Bank Thailand Office.

World Health Organization (1999). *Figures and facts about suicide.* Geneva: WHO.

Yip, P. S. F. (1998). Age, gender, marital status and suicides-An empirical study from East and West. *Psychological Reports,* 82, 311-322.

Yip, P. S. F. and Tan, R. C. E. (1998). Suicide in Hong Kong and Singapore: A tales of two cities. *International Journal of Social Psychiatry,* 44: 267–79.

Zhang, J., Conwell, Y., Zhou, L., et al. (2004). Culture, risk factors and suicide in rural China: A psychological autopsy case control study. *Acta Psychiatrica Scandinavica,* 110: 430–7.

Chapter 8 (Singapore)

Aaron, R., Joseph, A., Abraham, S., et al. (2004). Suicides in young people in rural southern India. *Lancet,* 35: 1117–8.

Barraclough, B. and Huges, J. (1987). *Suicide: Clinical and epidemiological studies.* London: Croom Helm Ltd (1st edition).

Boors, M. (1980). Relationship between employment rates and suicide rates in eight countries: 1962–1967. *Psychological Reports,* 47: 1095–1101.

Chia, B. H. (1978). Suicide in Singapore. MD thesis, University of Singapore.

Chia, B. H. and Tsoi, W. H. (1972). Suicide in Singapore. *Singapore Medical Journal,* 13(2): 91–7.

Chia, B. H. (2001). *Age of despair — A study of elderly suicide in Singapore.* Singapore: Times Books International.

Chia, B. H. Chia, A. & Tai, B. C. 2008, *Suicide letters in Singapore, Archive of Suicide Research,* 12: 74–81.

Danigelis, N. and Pope, W. (1969). Durkheim's theory of suicide as applied to the family: An empirical test. *Social Force,* 57:1081–1106.

Durkheim, E. (1951). Suicide — A study in sociology. Trans. J. A. Spaulding and G. Simpson G. London: Routledge and Kegan Paul Ltd.

Gist, R. and Welsh, Q. B. (1989). Certification change versus actual behavior changes in teenage suicide rates 1955–1979. *Suicide and Life-Threatening Behavior,* 19: 227–87.

Hassan, R. (1983). *A way of dying: Suicide in Singapore.* Oxford University Press.

Ho, S. F. (1985). *Suicides and weather in Singapore.* Assignment for Bachelor of Arts Degree, National University of Singapore.

Kakar, S (1978). *The inner world: A psychoanalysis study of childhood and society in Indian.* Oxford University Press.

Khan, M. M. (2002). Suicide on the Indian subcontinent. Crisis, 23(3): 104–7.

Ko, S. M. and Kua, E. H. (1995). Ethnicity and elderly suicide in Singapore. *International Psychogeriatrics*, 7(2): 309–17.

Kok, L. P. (1992). Suicidal behaviour in Singapore. In *Suicidal behaviour in the Asia-Pacific region*, ed. L. P. Kok and W. S. Tseng. Singapore University Press, National University of Singapore.

Kok, L.P. and Aw, S. C. (1992). Suicide in Singapore 1986. *Australia and New Zealand Journal of Psychiatry*, 25: 599–608.

Kua, E. H. and Sim, L. P. (1982). Suicide by psychiatric patients in *Singapore. Singapore Medical Journal*, 25(5): 252–4.

Leow, B. G. (2001). *Census of Population 2000: Demographic Characteristics*, Integrated Press Ptd. Ltd., Singapore.

Lloyd, C. J. and Yip, P. S. F. (2001). A comparison of suicide patterns in Australia and Hong Kong. *Journal of Royal Statistics Society*, 164(3): 467–83.

Luoma, J. U. B, Martin, C. E. and Pearson J. L. (2002). Contact with mental health and primary care providers before suicide: A review of the evidence. *American Journal of Psychiatry*, 159: 909–16.

Maaruf, S. (2004). *Some theoretical problems concerning tradition and modernization among Malays in Southeast Asia; in Asian traditions and modernization: Perspectives from Singapore*, ed. M. C. Yong. 208–28. Singapore: Eastern Universities Press.

Mehta, K. (1990). *Giving up hope: A study of attempted suicide amongst Indian women in Singapore.* Singapore: Times Book International.

Murphy, H. B. M. (1954). Mental health in Singapore: Suicide. *Medical Journal Malaya*, 9: 1–45.

Phillips, M. R., Li, X., and Zhang, Y. (2002). Suicide rates in China, 1995–99. *Lancet*,359: 835–40.

Overstone, I. M. K. (1973). A pschiatric approach to the diagnosis of suicide and its effect upon the Edinburh statistics. *British Journal of Psychiatry*; 123: 15–21.

Parker, G., Gao, F., and Machin, D. (2001). Seasonality of suicide in Singapore: Data from the equator. *Psychological Medicine*, 31: 549–53.

Purushotam, N. (2004). *The Singapore trader: The traditions of a modern economic sector; in Asian traditions and modernization: Perspectives from Singapore*, ed. M. C. Yong. 142–76. Singapore: Eastern Universities Press. :

Registry of Birth and Deaths (2004). *Report of Registration of Births and Deaths 2003*, Kai Hong Printing Service, Singapore.

Smith, J. C., Mercy, J. A., and Conn, J. M. (1988). Marital status and the risk of suicide. *American Journal of Public Health*, 78: 78.

Stack, S. (2000). Suicide: A 15-year review of the sociological literature part II: Modernization and social integration perspective. *Suicide and Life-Threatening Behavior*, 30(2): 163–76.

Singh, B. and Jenkins, R. (2000). Suicide prevention strategies — An international perspective. *International Review of Psychiatry*, 12: 7–14.

Ting, S. K. and Tan, K. K. (1969). Postmortem survey of suicide in Singapore. *Singapore Medical Journal*, 4: 248–58.

Toolan, J. M. (1962). Suicide and suicidal attempts in children and adolescents. *American Journal of Psychiatry*, 118: 719–24.

Tseng, W. S., Hsu, J., Omori, A., and Mclaughin, D. G. (1992). Suicidal behaviour in Hawaii, In *Suicidal behaviour in the Asia-Pacific region*, ed. L. P. Kok and W. S. Tseng.Singapore University Press, National University of Singapore..

Tsoi, W. F. and Chia, B. H. (1974). Suicide and mental illness in Singapore. *Singapore Medical Journal*, 15(3): 191–6.

Tsoi, W. F. and Kua, E. H. (1987). Suicide following parasuicide in Singapore. *British Journal of Psychiatry*, 151: 543–5.

WHO: Suicide Rates (n.d.), viewed March 2003, <http://www.who.int/mental_health/prevention/suicide/suiciderates/en>

Yeates, C., Duberstein, P. R., and Caine, E.D. (2005). Risk factors for suicide in later life. Biological Psychiatry, 52: 193–204.

Yip, P. S. F. (1998). Age, sex, marital status and suicide: An empirical study of East and West. *Psychological Reports*, 82: 311–22.

Yip, P. S. F and Thorburn, J. (2004). Marital status and the risk of suicide: Experience from England and Wales, 1982–1996. *Psychological Reports*, 94: 401–7.

Zhang, J,, Jia, S., Wieczorek, W, F, and Jiang, C. (2002). An overview of suicide research in China. *Archives of Suicide Research*, 6: 167–84.

Chapter 9 (India)

National Crime Research Bureau (2002). *Accidental Deaths and Suicide in India*. Ministry of Home Affairs, Government of India.

De Leo, D. (2003). The interface of schizophrenia, culture and suicide. In *Suicide Prevention: Meeting the challenge together*, ed. L. Vijayakumar. 11–41. Chennai, Orient Longman.

Gehlot, P. S., and Nathawat, S. S. (1983). Suicide and family constellation in India. *American Journal of Psychotherapy*, 37: 273–8.

Gururaj, G., Isaac, M., Subhakrishna, D. K. et al. (2004). Risk factors for completed suicide in a case-control study from Bangalore, India. *Injury Control and Safety Promotion*, 11: 183–91.

Hegde, R. S. (1980). Suicide in rural community. *Indian Journal of Psychiatry*, 22, 368–70.

Joseph, A., Abraham, S., Muliyil, J. P. et al. (2003). Evaluation of suicide rates in rural India using verbal autopsies, 1994–99. *British Medical Journal*, 326: 1121–22.

Latha, K.S., Bhat, S.M., D'Souza, P. (1996). Suicide attempters in a general hospital unit in India: Their socio-demographic and clinical profile — emphasis on cross-cultural aspects. *Acta Psychiatrica Scandinavica*, 94: 26–30.

Mayer, P. and Ziaian, T. (2002). Suicide, gender, and age variations in India. Are women in Indian society protected from suicide? *Crisis*, 3: 98–103.

Rao, A. V. (1991). Suicide in the elderly: A report from India. *Crisis*,12: 33–9.

Kumar Shuba, Jeyaseelan L, Suresh Saradha and Ahuja RC.(2005) Domestic Violence And Its Mental Health Correlates in Indian Women. *British Journal of Psychiatry*,

Srinivasan, T. N. and Thara, R. (2003). Schizophrenia patients who kill themselves. In *Suicide prevention: Meeting the Challenge Together*. ed. L. Vijayakumar. 163–8. Chennai, Orient Longman. .

Stone, G. D. (2002). Biotechnology and suicide in India. *Anthropology News*, May. http://artsci.wustl.edu/~anthro/research/biotech_suicide.html

Thakur, U. (1963). *The history of suicide in India.* 10–8. Delhi: Oriental Publishers.

World Health Organization. (2001). The World Health Report. 42.

Vijayakumar, L. and Thilothammal, N. (1993). Suicide pacts in India. *Crisis,* 14: 43–6.

Vijayakumar, L. and Rajkumar, S. (1999). Are risk factors for suicide universal? A case-control study in India. *Acta Pscyhiatrica Scandinavica,* 99: 407–11.

Vijayakumar, L. (2003). Psychosocial risk factors for suicide in India. In *Suicide prevention: Meeting the challenge together,* ed. L. Vijayakumar. 149–62. Chennai, Orient Longman.

Vijayakumar, L. (2004). Altruistic suicide in India. *Archives of Suicide Research,* 8: 73–80.

Vijayakumar, L. (2005a). Suicide in developing countries. Risk factors. *Crisis,* 26: 112–9.

Vijayakumar, L. (2005b). Suicide in developing countries. Prevention efforts. *Crisis,* 26(3): 120–4.

Chapter 10 (Conclusion and Reflections)

Centre for Suicide Research and Prevention (2005) *Research Findings into Suicide and its Prevention.* The University of Hong Kong, Hong Kong.

Chan, K. P. M., Yip, P. S. F., Au, J. and Lee, D. T. S. (2005). Charcoal-burning suicide in post-transition Hong Kong. *British Journal of Psychiatry,* 186: 67–73.

Chan, Wincy, Wong, P., Chen, E., and Yip, P. (2007). Suicide and unemployment — Missing link. *Archives of Suicide Research* 11, 1–9.

Chen, E. Y., Chan, W. S., Wong, P. W., et al. (2006). Suicide in Hong Kong: a case-control psychological autopsy study. *Psychological Medicine,* 36(6): 815–25.

Lewis, G., Hawton, K., Jones, P. (1997). Strategies for preventing suicides. *British Journal of Psychiatry,* 171:351–4.

Knox, K. L., Litts, D. A., Talcott, G. W., et al. (2003). Risk of suicide and related adverse outcomes after exposure to a suicide prevention program in the US Air Force: A cohort study. *British Medical Journal,* 327: 1376–80.

Liu, K. Y., Chen, E. Y., Chan, C. L., et al. (2006). Socio-economic and psychological correlates of suicidality among Hong Kong working age adults: Results from a population based study. *Psychological Medicine,* 36(6): 1759–67.

Liu, K. Y., Beautrais, A., Caine, E., et al. (2007). Charcoal burning suicides in Hong Kong and urban Taiwan: An illustration of the impact of a novel suicide method on overall regional rates. *Journal of Epidemiology Community Health,* 61: 248–53.

Phillips, M. R., Yu, X., Zhang, Y. (2002). Suicide rates in China 1995–1999. *Lancet;* 360: 835–40.

Rose, R. (1992). *The strategy of preventive medicine.* 24. Oxford University Press.

Wong, P. W. C., Liu, P. M. T., Chan, W. S. C., Law, Y. W., Law, C. K., Fu, K. W., Li, H. S. H., Tso, M. K., Beautries, A. L. and Yip, P. S. F. (2008). An integraative community-based prevention program for visitor charcoal-burning suicide and suicide pact. To appear in *Suicide and Life Threatening Behaviour.*

World Health Organization (2002). *World report on violence and health.* Geneva: WHO.

Yim, P., Yip, P., Li, R., et al. (2004). Suicide after discharge from psychiatric inpatient care: A case-control study in Hong Kong. *Australian and New Zealand Journal of Psychiatry,* 38: 65–72.

Yip, P. S. F., Liu, K. Y. Law, C. K., (2008). Years of Life Lost (YLL) due to suicide in China, 1990–2000. *Journal of Crisis Intervention and Suicide Prevention,* 29(3): 131–136.

Yip, P. S., Fu, K. W., Yang, K. C., et al. (2006). The effects of a celebrity suicide on suicide rates in Hong Kong. *Journal of Affective Disorders*, 93(1–3): 245–52.

Yip, P. S. F., Liu, K. Song, X. M. and Hu, J. P. (2005a). Suicide rate in China during a decade of rapid social changes. Social. *Psychiatric and Psychiatric Epidemiology*, 40: 792–8.

Yip, P. S. F., Liu, K. Y., Law, C. K. and Law, F. Y. W. (2005b). Social and economic burden of suicide in Hong Kong SAR. *Journal of Crisis Intervention and Suicide Prevention*, 26: 156–9.

Yip, P. S. F. (2005). A public health approach to suicide prevention. *Hong Kong Journal of Psychiatry*, 15: 29–31.

Yip, P. S. F. and Lee, D. T. S. (2007). Charcoal-burning suicides and strategies for prevention. *Journal of Crisis Intervention and Suicide Prevention*, 28: 21–27.

Index